Den HAAG Cook Book

A celebration of the amazing food & drink on our doorstep.

Den Haag Cook Book

©2018 Meze Publishing Ltd. All rights reserved.

First edition printed in 2018 in the UK.

ISBN: 978-1-910863-35-0

Thank you to: Marcel van der Kleijn

Compiled by: Anna Tebble, Casper Van Dort

Written by: Katie Fisher, Ella Michele

*Photography by: Casper van Dort
(www.cavado.nl)*

Edited by: Phil Turner

Designed by: Matt Crowder, Paul Cocker

*Contributors: Sarah Koriba, David Wilson,
Kym Du Toit*

*Cover art: David Broadbent
(www.davidbroadbent.co.uk)*

me:ze
PUBLISHING

Published by Meze Publishing Limited
Unit 1b, 2 Kelham Square
Kelham Riverside
Sheffield S3 8SD
Web: www.mezepublishing.co.uk
Telephone: 0114 275 7709
Email: info@mezepublishing.co.uk

FOREWORD

As the founder of four unique restaurants in the fascinating city of The Hague, I have achieved an ambition of mine to serve up a diverse variety of restaurant experiences.

I was born and raised in the rural province of Zeeland, but at heart I'm a real city man and The Hague is the ultimate destination for me. It has everything: beautiful museums, parks and rural areas, a bustling downtown, Holland's parliament and the Royal family, all in unique combination with the seaside and some fabulous beaches. Last but not least, there is a huge selection of restaurants with different styles of cuisine. The Hague really does offer something for everybody.

I've been a cook myself for more than 35 years, 25 of which have been spent as a chef in The Hague. This means that I've trained and 'raised' a lot of young talented cooks, and it's wonderful to see that a lot of them have since started their own restaurant in The Hague or nearby. Some have even become business partners in my restaurants, which you can read more about in this book.

When it comes to my own approach to food, I don't deny my heritage on the westernmost coastline of Holland, so fish and seafood will always be listed on my menus. Our restaurant garden, Laantje Voorham, is the cherry on top as it allows the chefs at Calla's, Oogst, BIT and Tapisco to use fresh herbs, flowers and vegetables during their best seasons.

Let's have a round of applause for all the amazing chefs and restaurants with their own vision and style who have contributed to this cook book, because I truly believe that when somebody said "if you succeed in building a successful company in The Hague, you can make it everywhere," they were right!

Marcel van der Kleijn

Hello from
DEN HAAG

The recipes featured in this book are a brilliant reflection of the diversity in the food and drink scene here, in the royal city of the Netherlands.

I was born and raised in Princenhage, a small neighbourhood in the city of Breda in the south of the Netherlands, as one of seven children (three brothers and three sisters). My mother didn't like to cook all the time, so around the age of 11 I happily took over the task of creating meals for us. Even then, I enjoyed experimenting with different recipes, which sometimes my family – who preferred to eat traditional food they recognised – weren't so keen on… several times I found that some of my more unusual ingredients had been hidden from me!

After attending hotel school, I moved to The Hague and began work as a wine merchant and supplier to the local restaurants. This was my career for more than 13 years, during which time I gained lots of knowledge about wine and food pairings. This was essential for advising customers in the shop, sommeliers and restaurant owners.

The Hague is a big city with a variety of neighbourhoods, each with its own sub-culture. I've had the opportunity to discover all the different restaurants and cooking styles during my years living here, and I believe that The Hague is now armed to do culinary battle with the big cities in the Netherlands, thanks to a stream of young entrepreneurs – each with their own philosophy and culinary concept – together with the city's well-known, established restaurants.

Last year I had the chance to explore Amsterdam through my camera lens, which was an amazing project to be part of in what was, for me personally, an undiscovered city. The result – The Amsterdam Cook Book – was amazing, so I'm very happy that The Hague's own version will be its successor, showcasing the culinary treasures of my chosen home town.

Enjoy the stories, visit the places, try the dishes, and I hope you get as much pleasure from perusing this book as I did compiling it.

Casper van Dort

CONTENTS

Royally signed, sealed, DELIVERED

André Kerstens is a family business with a long and illustrious history of importing and selling fine European wines.

Olaf Kerstens learnt everything he knows about wine from his father André, who, in his turn, had the reins handed to him by his father, and so on. In fact, the legacy of the business began in the 1600s, though the company as it exists today was established in 1880. André Kerstens BV is a wine importer with a shop selling to both wholesale and private individuals in The Hague, which Olaf opened in 2012 after joining the business in 1999. Olaf runs the shop with a team whose years of experience show there's a wealth of knowledge in-house.

They directly import from producers and prefers to work with family-run companies and co-operatives whose people are close to the decision making and therefore can form firm relationships. André Kerstens specialises in wines from three countries: Spain, France, and Portugal, and also includes a whole range of Port, sherry, Madeira and more. The shop also stocks plenty of spirits sourced from all over the world, which are always open for tasting and hark back to the days when Olaf's family produced their own spirits.

Since 1980 André Kerstens has had the title "By Appointment to the Court of the Netherlands". It is a seal of approval which can only come from the king and be awarded to family companies over a century old.

When people come into the shop, it's important to Olaf that their experience is very different from what you'd find in other wine stores and supermarkets. Attentive and personal service helps customers to match a wine with a meal, or pick a new favourite from the distinctive range the shop stocks. Olaf likes wines to represent the typical characters of their growing region, and tries to visit producers when he can to discover the best varieties so André Kerstens can act as a window for these great producers. An understanding of and passion for wine is needed to make a business really stand out, and with a reputation for quality passed down from generation to generation, Olaf and his family's business will be associated with expertise and great wines and spirits in The Hague for many years to come.

André Kerstens

ANDRE KERSTENS N.V.

WIJNEN - GEDISTILLEERD

TILBURG

André Kerstens

A SIX COURSE DINNER WITH OLAF AND HIS TEAM

One of the unique characteristics of our company is its diversity. The team have a wide range of ages, lifestyles, preferences, knowledge and characters. This makes each day, meeting, and dinner party dynamic. We would like to invite you to join us at the table and enjoy the six-course menu of wine pairings from our assortment.

DUTCH D-VINE
Dutch Flat Oysters with Lemon, Ginger, Passion fruit, Olive Oil

Made from the best Chardonnay and Pinot Noir fruit of the unique terroir of Avize in the Côte des Blancs region, all Frerejean Frères wines age for at least five years in their cellars. Packed with beautiful aromas of citrus and hints of roasted brioche and nuts. On the palate: elegant with nutty ripe notes and delicious small bubbles. The spicy notes of ginger and the fresh fruity accents of the lemon and passion fruit make this a perfect match with the saltiness and cucumber notes of the cultivated Dutch flat oysters.

Champagne Frerejean Frères, Brut 1er Cru

RAW REDEMPTION
Classic Ceviche

Located in the North-East of Spain, near San Sebastian, Bodega Gaintza produces this essential Spanish Basque Country wine mainly from Hondarrabi Zuri grapes. Traditionally, Txakolina is poured high above the glass so that natural CO_2 causes that typical milky appearance in the glass. Once in the glass, a fresh citrus nose shows a juicy, round palate with succulent lemon and stone fruit flavours. The refreshing acidity provides lift, freshness and length with a remarkable punchiness which matches the sour and herbal tones of a sea bass ceviche. For us, this pairing instantly brings a brilliant summer vibe to the table.

Bodega Gaintza, Getaria, Txakolina

FISH IN THE TREE
Lobster Risotto with Red Prawns, Bottarga

Quinta dos "Carvalhais" (Oak Trees) is renowned in the region for representing the art, authenticity and quality of the best Dão wines. This White Reserve honours the old traditions of the region in relation to aging white wines, which were commonly stored for long periods in old oak casks that were subject to variable environmental conditions throughout the year. The Branco Reserva shows a dense aroma with prominent buttery notes, hints of honey and citrus, mineral touches and a vegetal quality that adds both freshness and complexity. On the palate there is aromatic complexity bestowed by the oak barrels, alongside notes of fruit and honey that are perfectly balanced by a lively acidity. The intense umami richness of the bottarga and lobster, both used in the risotto, matches perfectly with the deep, aromatic, ripe, and complex tones of this great wine.

Quinta dos Carvalhais, Dão, Branco Reserva

RIDING THE LAMB
Saddle of Lamb with Herb Gravy, Green Lentils, Green Cabbage

For over 140 years, four generations of the López de Heredia family have devoted themselves to producing exceptional and unique wines. Vineyard care, a scrupulous selection of grapes, ageing in oak barrels in the heart of deep underground galleries, and the later ageing in bottles all contribute to making these illustrious wines with their exceptional bouquet. The Tempranillo-dominated Viña Tondonia Tinto Reserva reveals a light fresh texture with notes of vanilla and dried berry aromas with a rich, very dry, smooth, developed palate. With this, together with the firm tannins, the saddle of lamb feels very at home, leaving a complete, satisfying impression.

Bodegas Lopez de Heredia, Rioja, Viña Tondonia Tinto Reserva

FIGS DON'T FLY
Foie Gras with Shallot Gravy, Marinated Figs, Gingerbread-Cumin Crumble

Cossart Gordon & Co. was established in 1745, is the oldest company in the Madeira Wine trade and is to this day considered the very finest available. Cossart Gordon five year old Bual was aged in American oak casks in the traditional Canteiro system. This comprises the gentle heating of the wine in the lofts of the lodges in Funchal. Over the years the wine is transferred from the top floors to the middle floors and eventually to the ground floor where it is cooler. After this gradual 'estufagem' the wine undergoes racking and fining before the blend is assembled and bottled. This five year old Boal reveals a bouquet of dried fruit, vanilla, wood and toffee with a smooth, medium-sweet finish and an excellent balance between the fruit and acidity. The greasy, sweet and salty flavours of the foie gras dish combine perfect with the sweet but tangy notes of this remarkable Madeira wine.

Cossart Gordon, five year old Bual Madeira

FRENCH KISS…
Puff Pastry, Custard, Rhubarb, Wild Strawberries, Lemon Curd

Domaine du Petit Clocher is the work of four successive generations at Cléré Sur Layon, evolving for over 50 years. Being in the very heart of the roots of Chenin Blanc, hard work, knowledge and respect for the country resulted in very high quality wines which can be found on the world's greatest wine lists. Powerful and balanced, with exotic aromas of pineapple and lychee. Sweet, but not sticky, with a beautiful richness which accompanies the custard and boosts the extravagant flavours of the wild strawberries even more, leaving the lemon curd and the rhubarb to freshen up the palate. The perfect kiss for the wine and the dish.

Domaine du Petit Clocher, Coteaux du Layon, Les Perrières

AFTER DINNER:
Small talk, laughter and some heated discussions…

At the end of the meal, we keep the table occupied, walking around and switching seats. The wine and food combinations are discussed and new combinations are devised, jokes are made and there is discussion about what is going on in the business. The evening ends after everyone has drunk their last glass. Wine, coffee, cognac, digestives and beer are on the table.

Thank you for your company, and good night for now!

297,-   234,-   166,50

The art OF GRILLING

The name of BIT – which stands for 'Best in Town' – tells you almost everything you need to know about what the grill and café aims to achieve in The Hague!

BIT Grill & Café is owned and run by Marcel van de Kleijn, who is also the restaurant's head chef. He opened the second of his three businesses in The Hague during 2014, and named it BIT – which stands for 'Best In Town' – because that encompasses everything it stands for and what the team aim to achieve. Kilian has been the general manager since 2016 and has built up a core team who are committed to maintaining the high standards of food and service.

Located inside the oldest four star hotel in The Hague, BIT is all about good food in a cosy and informal atmosphere for a wide variety of visitors from every age group and nationality. They even regularly welcome guests from abroad who return to visit them! Natural materials – wood, brick, and stone – give the interior a classic yet contemporary feel, and the restaurant is designed so that guests can sit around a long wooden refectory table in a large group or in a quiet corner for a business meeting. The bar serves good wines, gins, snacks and the terrace is "the most beautiful in the city, even though I am a little biased!" according to

Kilian, set amidst the historical architecture with the parliament buildings in view.

The main draw at the grill and café is, of course, the charcoal-fired Josper grill in the centre of the dining space: perfect for cooking the juiciest, most flavoursome, prime cuts of meat. Burgers, rib roasts, steaks and daily specials including flammkuchen and seafood come straight to the table from the sizzling hot grill which is on show in the open kitchen.

Everything is made in-house, from sauces to salads and other accompaniments, and the butchery is cleaned in-house as well to ensure the meat is top quality. The beef comes from Ireland, and for the steaks only Hereford cattle are used, bought directly from the importer. Trimmings are used too so the restaurant can be as environmentally friendly as possible... a challenge for the team with meat as their speciality but one they embrace anyway! Marcel's concept is based on excellent quality and a laid-back place to eat out with style and class, and as Kilian says, above all BIT is "set apart by the meat that we serve – it's the best in town!"

BIT Grill & Café

BIT Grill & Café
RIB ROAST WITH BÉARNAISE SAUCE

The perfect pick from our Josper grill: a prime rib roast best served from a searing hot grill with fresh pepper and a good pinch of salt. This Hereford roast is an excellent recipe all year round once you've mastered the cooking itself. Make sure to visit your local butcher for the best meat in town and don't be shy with the seasoning.

Preparation time: 15 minutes | Cooking time: 30-45 minutes | Serves: 2-3

Ingredients

For the rib roast:

1kg rib on the bone (don't forget you are losing about 10% while cooking and one bone weighs around 150g)

Salt and pepper

Splash of oil (preferably grape oil)

For the béarnaise sauce:

175g butter

4 egg yolks

15ml white wine

15ml white wine vinegar

Salt and pepper

Tarragon, finely chopped

Method

Make sure that the meat is at room temperature, and then season the rib roast on both sides and leave for 10 minutes. Sear the meat in a pan with the oil on a medium heat until all sides are light brown in colour. Place in a preheated oven at 140°c for 18 minutes. Take the meat out of the oven and put it aside to rest for the same amount of time to ensure that the steak is succulent and tender.

Meanwhile, heat up a barbecue (preferably a closed circuit) and maintain a minimum temperature of 220°c. Prepare the béarnaise sauce while it's heating up.

For the béarnaise sauce

For a smooth sauce, completely melt the butter on very low heat and set aside. Then mix the egg yolks, white wine, white wine vinegar, pepper, and salt in a bowl and whisk for 15-20 minutes in a bain-marie. Make sure the bowl does not touch the water to avoid ending up with scrambled eggs. When the egg mixture begins to thicken to a yoghurt-like consistency, gently add the melted butter and add tarragon according to preference. Set the sauce aside while you finish the rib roast.

For a perfect medium-rare steak, put the rib roast on the barbecue and sear for 1 minute and 30 seconds, then turn 45 degrees for a nice diamond-shaped pattern on the meat. Repeat this on the other side. This should take about 6 minutes on the barbecue; 3 on each side. Leave to rest in some foil for a couple of minutes. If you like to begin your evening with a starter, you can prepare both the meat and the sauce in advance. However, don't forget to gently heat the sauce using a bain-marie while whisking to avoid any lumps, and make sure that the meat has a core temperature of 45°c before putting it onto the barbecue, otherwise you'll end up with a cold steak!

To serve

If you'd like to show off, prepare the rib roast on a wooden or stone meat board and garnish with grilled tomatoes, onions and fried laurel. A good alternative is to use grilled sweetcorn, or try puffed garlic if you like the flavour. Serve with chips or a baked potato, and a fresh salad.

The buzz of
THE BISTRO

The international style of food served at Restaurant Basaal reflects the vibrant fusion of cultures, flavours and produce that make The Hague's food and drink scene so appealing.

Restaurant Basaal is not only an integral part of The Hague's neighbourhood, but belongs to a wider community that shines through in the food and atmosphere at the popular dining destination. The owner, Bas Oonk, began working in the hospitality industry at the age of 17 so has plenty of experience to draw on. He aims for the restaurant to use as much local produce as possible and combines Dutch cuisine with French-style cooking as well as Indonesian influences. The menu keeps updating with the times, but some signature dishes – the chicken liver with bacon, caramelised shallots and Port sauce is a particular favourite with customers – have been served up since day one. Fresh fish, brought straight from the nearby harbour to Basaal's kitchen, features in lots of the dishes to showcase the best you can get when it comes to fresh ingredients.

Bas still oversees the cooking himself, but has brought a great team together who maintain the high standards Restaurant Basaal has always upheld. He also set up and still participates in a chef's exchange at his restaurant to encourage the mingling of different cuisines from around the world, giving Basaal's chefs the opportunity to cook and learn abroad. Other chefs from various countries join Bas' kitchen too, bringing their expertise and passion for the food and drink of other cultures into The Hague. Basaal's sous chef, Roman Mikuliča, is from the Czech Republic; he and Bas met on an exchange which shows just how fruitful they can be after five years of the successful venture.

Open since 2001, Basaal brings history and modernity together too. The 18th century building that houses the restaurant sits on the banks of a canal in one of only a few truly authentic areas. It used to be used as storage for beer, so it's fitting that the grand exterior still promises great local produce for residents and tourists. From the Bib Gourmand and Chef's Menus to its beautiful setting in the centre of The Hague, Bas ensures that his restaurant has lots to offer for anyone who enjoys great food from their home country with a twist of innovative, international flavour.

BASAAL

Restaurant Basaal

CROQUETTES OF FRESH WATER CRAYFISH

These croquettes are a modern take on a typical Dutch classic. They have been on the menu at Restaurant Basaal for over 10 years.

Preparation time: 3 hours 30 minutes | Cooking time: 30 minutes | Makes: 14

Ingredients

For the croquettes:

75g butter

80g Calabrian chilli peppers in oil, deseeded and chopped

5 cloves of garlic, crushed

120g flour

300ml shrimp stock

2 leaves of gelatine, soaked in cold water

500g fresh water crayfish tails, roughly chopped

½ bunch of flat leaf parsley, chopped

100g flour

4 eggs, beaten

1 bag of panko breadcrumbs

For the saffron mayonnaise:

Pinch of saffron powder

4 tbsp white wine vinegar

½ clove of garlic

2 egg yolks

Salt and pepper

250ml sunflower oil

Squeeze of lemon juice

Method

For the croquettes

Make a roux by melting the butter in a pan over a gentle heat and combining it with 15ml of the oil from the chilli peppers. Brown the crushed garlic in the roux and then remove the garlic and stir in the flour. Continue to stir gently until the roux is shiny. Add the shrimp stock to the roux and slowly bring up to boiling point. Keep stirring to avoid burning. Add the soaked gelatine to the mixture and then leave it to cool for 30 minutes. Now add the fresh water crayfish tails, chilli peppers and the chopped flat leaf parsley. Chill this for 1 hour in the fridge.

When cold, roll the mixture into small croquettes by hand. Each one should be approximately 45 grams. Roll the shaped croquettes in the flour first, then dip each one in beaten egg and coat in Panko breadcrumbs. Ideally, rest the croquettes for a couple of hours in the fridge (or make them the day before and chill overnight). To cook, deep-fry the croquettes at 180°c for 3 minutes until golden.

For the saffron mayonnaise

Soak the saffron powder in the white wine vinegar at least 1 hour before making the mayonnaise. Mix this with the garlic, egg yolks, salt and pepper in a food processor and blitz until you get a paste. Slowly add the sunflower oil while blending to get a mayonnaise. Flavour with salt, pepper and lemon juice.

To serve

Garnish the dish with a green salad and deep-fried parsley leaves.

Journey of
DISCOVERY

Bites & Stories is a walking food tour showcasing Den Haag's eclectic collection of food and drinks alongside tales of historical significance, royal approval and unrivalled flavour.

The top three priorities for a visitor in a new city are food, walking, and discovering… this was the first thing that Kerensa van der Sluys found out when she heard about the concept of food tours and decided to bring one to her home city. Kerensa grew up in The Hague and was surprised when her initial research revealed that no food tours existed there, which prompted the enterprising then-PhD student to start her own company, Bites & Stories.

The growing company was aptly named from the beginning; Kerensa takes a small group (usually 8-10 people) around the city by way of various snacks and treats from participating businesses – the bites – while regaling them with fascinating facts and histories – the stories – of the food and drink stops in question, which vary according to the type of tour you choose. There's also a fair bit of sightseeing along the way, of course, as visitors discover The Hague in the best way: on foot, expertly guided by Kerensa herself or a similarly passionate and informed member of the team.

Developing the tours initially required the best kind of research; walking the proposed route herself and

checking out the foodie stops along the way! Kerensa had certain places in mind but wanted to make sure that the walk to link them showed off her city to its best advantage. She was very pleased to find that everyone she explained her idea to was really enthusiastic about getting involved. Since the first official tour in September 2015 Kerensa has been fine tuning the routes and expanding her incredibly successful venture to suit a variety of occasions and visitors.

"I'm so awed by and proud of the acknowledgement the tours have received in the last few years," she says. "The reviews from our customers have been a huge part of Bites & Stories' success."

There are now three main tours that people can book onto via the Bites & Stories website: Food, Wine, and a brand new Beer edition. There's also ample opportunity to tailor tours to a particular occasion – great for celebrating a food, wine or beer-lover's birthday – with the private group options for which Kerensa and her team will happily customise a tour to suit individual requirements (great for vegetarians, those who avoid gluten, or alcohol-free partying, for example).

PASSAGE

The Food tour is all about giving visitors an insight into the city life and daily eats of a resident from Den Haag. One of Kerensa's favourite stops on this route is a traditional butcher's shop by the name of Dungelmann which has existed since 1861. Set up by two brothers, the family business originally comprised one butcher and one cobbler on the same street. The cobbler developed into a chain of popular shoe shops but the butcher stayed local, known for its outstanding quality, with just one venue still serving favourites including their original recipe kroketten and meatballs which tour guests get to try. Places like this, admittedly not all with 'court deliverer' status – a seal of approval which can only come from the king and be awarded to family companies over a century old – as Dungelmann has retained over the years, are really special and unique to The Hague. Kerensa wouldn't consider her food tour complete without them!

The Wine tour takes a refreshing approach to tasting and discovering new and old favourites. "Drinking wine is normally all about learning in quite a serious and formal way, and our tour is the opposite of that," says Kerensa. "It's all about enjoying ourselves!" The tour features fewer stops to allow a more relaxed pace – and less walking after a glass or two – between the restaurants that feature. The emphasis, as with all the tours, is on places that might otherwise be missed by visitors to The Hague. The guides are of course integral to this approach; Kerensa ensures that each one is well matched to the tour they run and really does love the area.

This means that those hosting Bites & Stories newer Beer tour are in a perfect position to show off The Hague's breweries and craft beer cafés with genuine enthusiasm! All the beers tried on the tour have Dutch origins, and some come with legends of their very own. Eiber names its beers after The Hague's stories, such as 'The Baron' in which flavours of caramelised coffee candy – accidentally created for and then much loved by a real Baron in The Hague centuries ago – take centre stage, paying homage to the brewers' inspirations. The social element of beer drinking plays a big part in the history and recent innovations of Dutch brewing; Kompaan is the name of a very successful local brewery, which is an older Dutch word for friend, and even the most unlikely of places – a monastery with a tiny brewing kitchen in the centre of the city – encourages 'drinking with your brothers' in the case of the monks' popular sharing bottles of beer.

Kerensa has plans to expand her business in the near future, with ambitions to run food and drink tours in other Dutch cities as well as taking the Bites & Stories model to places that deserve their own culinary scene to be celebrated by similarly enthusiastic locals with their own drive to set up a neighbourhood or city tour, who could benefit from the expertise that Kerensa has built up. So look out for dedicated foodies coming to a place near you, and next time you visit The Hague make sure you eat, walk and discover everything this city of bites and stories has to offer!

Boulevard BURGERS

On the picturesque Strandweg Boulevard, Brooklyn is a favourite with tourists and locals alike for its classic American feel and inventive takes on classic burgers and steaks.

Brooklyn is one of four restaurants owned by good friends Preshaan and Leonard, and shares a distinctive character as well as the Strandweg Boulevard with Oceans Beach House. It opened in 2015 and pays homage to Preshaan's love of New York's eclectic culture as well as the pair's love of American style food. As the only burger and steak restaurant along the beach front, Brooklyn stands out straight away. The décor is equally inspired by Preshaan's travels to America, with cladding and warm lighting reminiscent of everything we've come to love about American food and dining. Designed to feel like a traditional steakhouse, Brooklyn pairs a warm welcome and buzzing atmosphere with food you can't wait to get stuck in to, making it a perfect slice of America in the heart of Den Haag.

Recognising the Dutch origins of the American borough of Brooklyn, Preshaan and Leonard's restaurant brings the best of the two destinations that inspire it together. While Den Haag is a city renowned for its sense of tradition, Brooklyn also reflects its multicultural community and thirst for innovative cuisine. This is echoed in the food and drink menus, which feature flavours from all around the world. Burgers with an Argentinian or Mexican twist sit alongside a few Dutch dishes that traditional, homely Scheveningen is known for. There's even an insect burger for those in search of real culinary adventure! Steaks from prime cuts, vegetarian burgers and fish dishes complete a line-up that aims to please everybody.

With their finger on the pulse, Brooklyn's kitchen team are always playing with new flavours and unique ingredients to make their Burgers of the Month and impress even their most regular local customers with an ever-evolving offering. Simply put, Preshaan and Leonard believe that the best meals are made from the finest quality ingredients. This ethos, in combination with an American lager or two and sunset on the boulevard makes Brooklyn a must visit for The Hague's Dutch residents and international visitors. The casual, easy-going approach to eating out has wide appeal; good burgers and steaks, beer, and good vibes are the key ingredients for a great time as far as Brooklyn's team are concerned and they're happy to keep up the good work for a long time yet!

Brooklyn
THE BROOKLYN BURGER

This really is one of the best burgers in Scheveningen! The patties are big, with melted cheddar cheese and bacon on top plus a spicy mayo sauce. Because we are the only burger restaurant in Scheveningen, we want to serve the best quality and surprisingly big burgers to our guests.

Preparation time: 10 minutes | Cooking time: 10 minutes | Serves: 1

Ingredients

1 onion

Splash of vegetable oil

2 tsp oregano

2 sprigs of coriander

½ tsp paprika

1 tsp each salt and pepper

200g ground beef

1 slice of cheddar cheese

3 rashers of bacon

½ lettuce

1 tomato

1 pickle

1 tbsp mayo

1 tbsp chilli sauce

1 burger bun

2 potatoes

Method

Cut the onion into rings and cook in a frying pan with a little vegetable oil and the oregano, coriander, paprika, salt and pepper for 2 minutes. Meanwhile, preheat the oven to 180˚c.

Shape the beef into a burger patty and then grill or fry for 3 minutes (1 minute 30 seconds per side) until medium. Top the beef with cheese and bacon and then place into the preheated oven for 5 minutes. Cut the lettuce, tomato, and pickle into pieces to add later. Combine the mayo and chilli sauce to taste for your own burger sauce. Spread this on the top half of the burger bun, add the bacon and cheese-topped burger and then the onion rings. Add the tomato, lettuce and pickles according to your liking.

For the French fries, peel the potatoes and then cut into 1cm slices, pile them on top of each other and cut them in 1cm slices again. Preheat the deep fat fryer or a pan of oil to 200˚c and then add the fries and cook for about 4 minutes until golden and crispy.

To serve

Serve the assembled burger with the hot French fries and tuck in!

Watching the world GO BY

Café Franklin is the contemporary hub of its bustling neighbourhood, putting flavours from around the world, local and international beers, and relaxed socialising on the menu.

Bas and Jan-Willem both studied economics and worked a lot in bars and restaurants during their studies, which is where their passion for hospitality started. Their first entrepreneurial adventure was Beachclub Indigo, a collaboration with good friends and a huge success! Two years later, Bas and Jan-Willem saw a new opportunity in the old city centre of The Hague and Walter Benedict was born. This new style brasserie became an instant hit, so after another two years they spotted a beautiful building on the other side of town and went for it. In spring 2015, Franklin opened its doors.

Franklin is a laid-back establishment, which has proved very popular for both locals and visitors to meet, chat, and people-watch through the spectacular floor-to-ceiling windows. From drinks to dinner and into the night, Franklin is "all about the view" – in the beautiful interior with quirky touches to the stylish décor, or from the pavement-side tables – combined with a mouth-watering choice of food and drinks. Made in-house, and much of it grilled on the Big Green Egg

barbecue, international influences pepper the menus, which feature fresh fish, healthy salads, steaks and burgers. Asian, South American and European staples are all complemented by a generous range of beers that Franklin has picked to represent established and small-scale local brewing. Guests can enjoy a drink until late any day of the week.

The team is proud to welcome a diverse mix of guests from young to old, people from the neighbourhood to expats, and foodies to business people who come in and enjoy the offering. "Setting up a place that lasts for decades and grows with the highly evolving hospitality scene, as well as continuously meeting and exceeding guest expectations... that for us is real success. Hospitality is a team sport and therefore it is highly fulfilling when we as a team make a lot of people happy."

Walter Benedict and Café Franklin are the products of a genuine wish to provide people with somewhere inviting that can boast a great atmosphere, which brings a neighbourhood together over tasty food and drink!

Café Franklin

Photography by Myrthe Slootjes

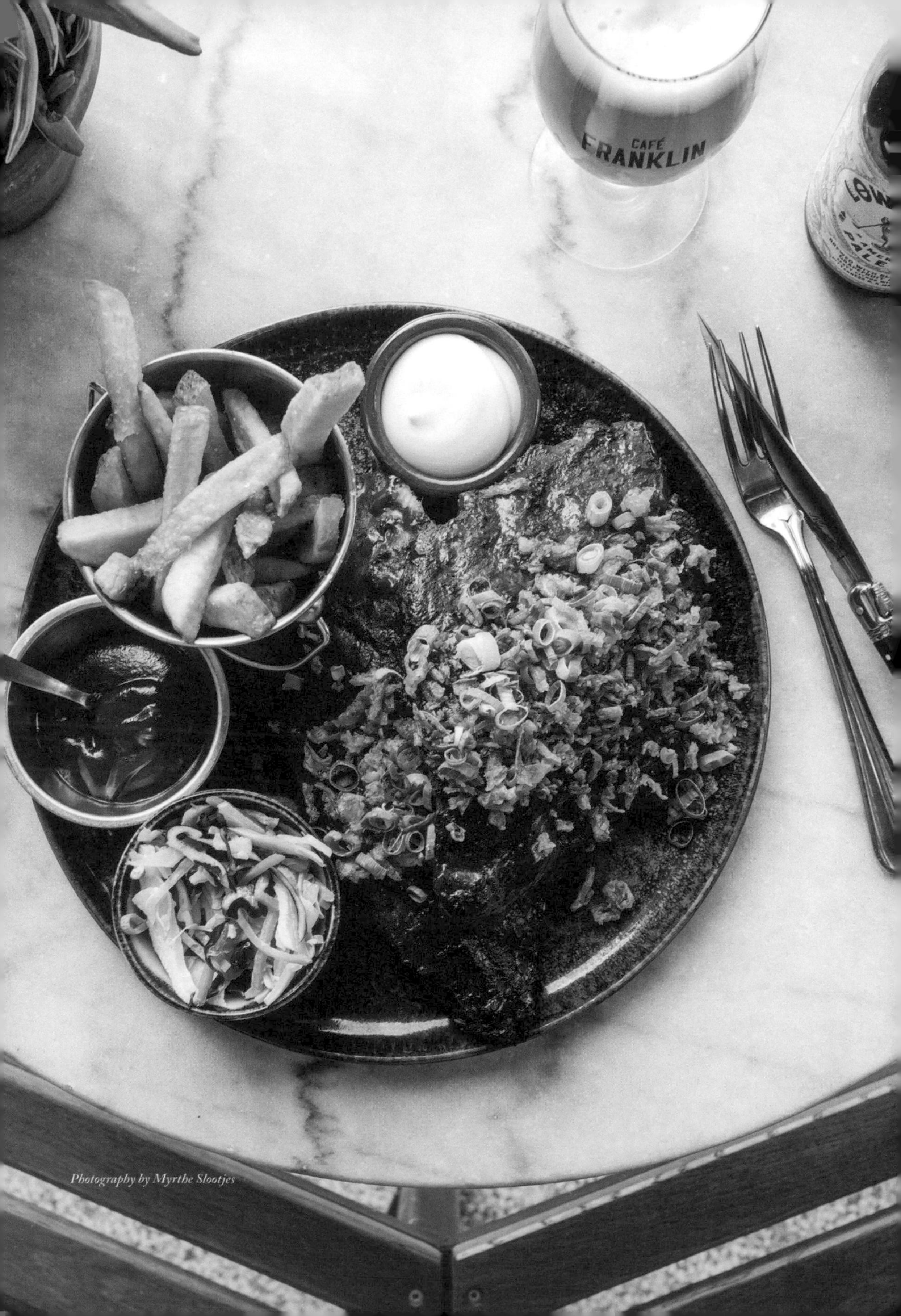

Photography by Myrthe Slootjes

Café Franklin
SPARE RIBS

Who doesn't like a good sticky pork rib? It may be a more challenging recipe for the standard home cook, but the hard work pays off!

Preparation time: 15 minutes | Cooking time: approx. 10 hours | Serves: 4

Ingredients

4kg good quality spare ribs

150g paprika powder

150g chilli powder

150g fennel seeds

For the BBQ paste:

80g fresh ginger

4 pieces of lemongrass

2 shallots

½ a chilli

150g apple syrup

2 litres ketchup

For the coleslaw:

100g carrot

100g white cabbage

100g red cabbage

60g raisins

3 tbsp crème fraîche

3 tbsp yoghurt

1 tbsp natural vinegar

2 tbsp mustard

1 lemon, juiced

Salt and pepper

For the garnish:

2 spring onions, sliced

200g crispy fried onion

Method

Start by making the dry rub. Mix the paprika powder, chilli powder and fennel seeds in a bowl and then massage the mixture onto your spare ribs. Put the spare ribs in a vacuum pack bag and seal. Place the ribs in a sous vide machine for 9-10 hours at 80°c. (If you don't have a sous vide machine, you can put the ribs in a pan filled with water over gentle heat but make sure the temperature stays at 80°c the whole time.)

For the BBQ paste

Meanwhile, cut the ginger, lemongrass, shallots and chilli into medium-sized pieces. Put them into a pan and stir-fry gently until everything is golden brown. Add the apple syrup and ketchup and let the mixture simmer for 3 hours to thicken up. Sieve the mixture to get a paste and set aside.

For the coleslaw

Cut the carrot, white and red cabbage into fine julienne. Mix with the raisins, crème fraîche, yoghurt, vinegar, mustard and lemon juice. Add salt and pepper to taste.

To bring everything together, get the barbecue ready for cooking on while the paste cooks. When it's ready, spread a generous amount of paste over the ribs (make sure you put enough on otherwise the ribs will dry out). Put the ribs on your barbecue and cook, turning occasionally, until they are hot and have a good browned barbecue edge!

To garnish

Garnish the spare ribs with spring onion and crispy fried onion. Serve with the coleslaw and french fries.

Growing CHANGES

Michelin-starred since 2002, Restaurant Calla's is a haven of fresh seasonal ingredients and fine dining in the city.

Restaurant Calla's was established in 1998 by Marcel van der Kleijn, and has been at the heart of fine dining in The Hague, long recognised for the quality and refinement of its cuisine. It's now co-owned by head chef Ronald van Roon and the restaurant's maître d' Bianca Fellinger, who are also husband and wife. Ronald's cooking style is simple yet full of flavour, putting the best produce he can source centre stage, which in many cases comes fresh from the restaurant's own garden. His ambition is to continue improving everything about Calla's – including working towards a second Michelin star – and to put The Hague well and truly on the map when it comes to fine dining in the city.

Ronald worked his way up through the kitchen at Calla's, having written to Marcel with a desire to expand his experience in a Michelin-level environment. It all started with an internship in a restaurant (which, incidentally, his grandfather lived next door to and was a regular guest at) where Ronald decided to become a chef. Today he is excited to develop and evolve his restaurant's offering, which comprises a four course and seven course menu, both changed five times a year in accordance with the availability of the very freshest produce. Ronald and the team are keen growers of unusual herb, vegetable and salad varieties, which they pick every morning to use in the cassoulet special – newly created each day depending on what's looking the nicest! – and the season's dishes.

The combination of traditional Dutch regional cuisine and Ronald's contemporary approach is reflected in the service and unique dining space at Calla's. This is both literal and figurative; mirrored walls give an illusion of space when in fact the restaurant is relaxed and intimate – there are only nine tables on the first floor, and one chef's table on the ground floor – but creates a real spectacle too. Waiters bring the diners their courses on silver platters directly from the kitchen via the central staircase, and Calla's sommelier is on hand to provide the perfect match to each mouthful.

Classic yet modern, refined yet exciting, small yet ambitious. In the capable hands of its experienced chef and maître d' Restaurant Calla's strives to be an example of how good urban Dutch dining can be, with the regional influences and emphasis on fresh ingredients that set its food apart, and a style that lives up to the beauty from which its name is derived.

Restaurant Calla's
'OOSTERSCHELDE' LOBSTER, WHITE ASPARAGUS AND 'ANNA DUTCH' CAVIAR

This is the epitome of a Dutch plate. Chef Ronald uses beautiful produce from the Netherlands; lobster from the Oosterschelde, white asparagus from the Brabantse Wal, 'Anna Dutch' caviar from Eindhoven and Calla's own regional vegetable garden for flowers, leaves and herbs.

Preparation time: approx. 20 minutes | Cooking time: approx. 10 minutes | Serves: 4

Ingredients

8 spears of white asparagus

1 lemon

2 Oosterschelde lobsters (500g each)

To garnish:

2 radishes

15g Anna Dutch caviar

4 green strawberries

Salt and pepper

Oxalis leaves

Arugula

Tatsoi

Vinaigrette

Method

Peel the asparagus, put them in a pan and cover with water and a pinch of salt. Bring to the boil. After boiling, remove the pan from the heat and let the asparagus cool off in the liquid.

Boil a large pan of water with a slice of lemon. Put the lobsters in the pan and cook for 5 minutes.

Drain the lobsters and rinse until cold. Remove the lobster meat from the shell, including the claws and tail.

To garnish

While preparing and plating, keep in mind circles and triangles to create balance in your presentation. Cut the radish into thin slices and place in iced water until you are ready to plate. Cut each asparagus spear into three equal pieces and each lobster into twelve pieces. Divide these between the plates, placing six pieces of asparagus and six pieces of lobster on each. Distribute the caviar over the plates with a small spoon to create three dots per person. Cut the strawberries into thin slices and spread over the plates. Dry the radish slices on paper towels and season with salt and pepper. Arrange on the plates. Garnish the plates with the oxalis leaves, arugula and tatsoi. Before serving the dish, finish each plate with a little drizzle of vinaigrette.

Something old, something NEW

Restaurant de Tapperij is one of The Hague's oldest café restaurants, established in 1886 at the heart of the stately Archipel neighbourhood.

For more than 20 years, Restaurant de Tapperij's owner and chef Hans Richel and his team have been cooking classic French-Mediterranean cuisine with a modern influence. His style evolved out of his experience working at renowned establishments such as Hotel des Indes, Saur, House of Lords and Bistroquet, all of which were leading lights of The Hague's culinary scene in their day. After years of wandering, Hans stepped into de Tapperij on the 1st December 1995 and thought "this will become my business". In just a few years, he transformed the ordinary neighbourhood pub into a renowned restaurant. Guests from all over the region found their way to de Tapperij, and the restaurant has become one of the classics in The Hague.

The food at de Tapperij is based on daily seasonal ingredients, and Hans has been working with the same local suppliers for many years to source the kitchen's groceries, fish and meat. Poultry and game are supplied by local hunters in the region, and during the game season, de Tapperij is well known for its good old-fashioned dishes: wild pigeon breast, venison steak, roasted pheasant, and slow-cooked game stew are just a few examples. The menu is on a large chalkboard, and the staff explain to guests what's on for the day, as dishes change weekly based on the ingredients available, though several 'classics' will be on the menu during the whole year, such as the very popular steak tartare and homemade shrimp croquettes.

The wine list is brief but versatile, showcasing well-known grape varieties, wine regions and producers. De Tapperij works with a select few of the area's wine merchants who fit this niche, including Bart Wijnen, Wijnkoperij de Gouden Ton, Wijn op Dronk and André Kerstens. The interior of de Tapperij nods to the 19th century when the famous writer Louis Couperus was a regular customer. The touches of nostalgia take you back to your grandmother's time; old paintings and antique Balinese masks hang on the walls, and the cupboard behind the bar is full of old bottles of genever, the Dutch national spirit from which modern-day gin evolved. The backroom where the 'Heerenkamer' is situated is perfect for private dinners and groups of up to 18, so whether you're celebrating an occasion or wanting to enjoy a sophisticated evening out, the past and present meet perfectly at Restaurant de Tapperij.

De Tapperij

De Tapperij
STEAK TARTARE

Steak Tartare is one of those dishes which will remain on our menu for years. The 'secret' of a great steak tartare is the method of preparing it; the meat is cut or sliced by hand, not by machine, so the taste is totally different.

Preparation time: 15 minutes | Serves: 4

Ingredients

400g ground steak or beef clod

1 tbsp chopped chives

1 tbsp capers

1 tbsp finely chopped onion

1 tbsp finely chopped pickled cucumber

1 tbsp mustard

4 egg yolks

Dash of Tabasco and Worcestershire sauce

Salt and pepper

To garnish:

Rocket salad

4 slices of good bread, toasted

Method

Take the meat out of the fridge 30 minutes before preparation, to allow it to become room temperature. Cut the meat into thin slices and then into small cubes using a very sharp knife. Mix the finely cut meat with the chives, capers, onion, pickled cucumber, mustard and egg yolk in a bowl, combining until it all comes together. Season with Tabasco, Worcestershire sauce, salt and pepper.

To garnish

Shape the tartare as desired in the centre of the plate. Garnish with rocket salad and a sprinkle of coarsely ground black pepper. Serve with toasted bread.

The perfect MATCH

Didong brings the best of its Den Haag community and Indonesian flavours together for everyone to enjoy, no matter what age or background.

The story of Didong began 20 years ago when Harry first met Fleur in an Indonesian restaurant. Fast-forward eight years; the couple's passion for food that both looks and tastes fantastic gave life to their own restaurant in the heart of Den Haag. Inhabiting a space that was once home to two previous Indonesian businesses that made their own mark on the neighbourhood, Didong is a part of a larger thriving Indonesian community in one of the city's older, yet vibrant northern quarters. Literally meaning 'stubborn', Harry and Fleur chose the name Didong not just because of its catchiness but because they also admire the sentiment of cooking with a sense of stubbornness; uncompromised quality, caring about the detail, and pride in the food you present to other people.

Although tradition and authenticity strongly feature in all their dishes, Didong's interior feels comfortably modern and fresh, as the couple wanted the spirit of Indonesia to be reflected in the food rather than old-fashioned batik décor. Seating up to 50 people, the restaurant is busy but intimate, with local regulars either taking their dinners home or to opting sit and enjoy Didong's buzzing atmosphere. This balance of old and new is achieved by Harry and his years of practice within the industry, but also with the help of chef Muslim who hails from Sumatra, and a team of mixed age and experience. Harry and Fleur describe Didong as "a place that you can take your old Indonesian aunt, but also your young niece" because it welcomes everyone with this diversity.

As part of its engagement with the Den Haag community, Didong strives to source produce solely from the Netherlands, or import ingredients from Indonesia itself. An example of this includes their famous roasted Babi Pangang, where the traditional Indonesian recipe is married with pork from Limburg, creating a match made in heaven. Catering both for those who love their spice and others with milder tastes, Didong's frequently changing specials reflect a hunger for new and innovative food, while also keeping the classics you can't help but order upon every visit. It's in the quality of ingredients, and the love that they put into every meal that Harry and Fleur believe give Didong its inslag: a heartfelt Indonesian word that is only used to describe something special that has genuine character, soul, mind and heart.

Didong
SAMBAL GORENG TELOR AND KANGKUNG KATJANG

This is a recipe for boiled egg in spicy coconut sauce with kangkung, a very popular vegetable in Asia. You can usually buy it at the market, but wild spinach would be a good alternative. Any unfamiliar ingredients should be easy to find in an Asian supermarket.

For the Sambal goreng telor: Preparation time: 5-10 minutes | Cooking time: 30 minutes | Serves: 6-8

For the Kangkung katjang: Preparation time: 5-10 minutes | Cooking time: 5-10 minutes | Serves: 4-6

Ingredients

For the Sambal goreng telor:

1.5 litres of water

2 medium-sized onions, diced

1 clove of garlic, diced

3 daun salam (leaves)

5cm laos (Siamese ginger), cut in half

1 sereh (lemongrass), bruised

2 djeroek poeroet leaves (lime leaves)

½ tsp white pepper

1 tbsp sugar

2–3 tbsp sambal oelek

1 tsp koenjit (turmeric powder)

2 packets (200g) of santen (concentrated coconut)

To finish:

Boiled eggs (1–2 per person)

Leek, thinly sliced

Celery leaf, sliced

Bawang goreng (fried onions)

For the Kangkung katjang:

2 tbsp vegetable oil

2 medium-sized onions, diced

1 clove of garlic, diced

1 tsp trassi bakar (shrimp powder)

1kg kangkung, washed and sliced

Salt, to season

2 red chilli peppers, cut and deseeded

A handful of peanuts, fried and finely chopped

Method

For the Sambal goreng telor

Heat the water in the pan with all the ingredients except the sambal oelek, koenjit and santen. When it boils, add the sambal badjak, koenjit and santen. Bring back to the boil and stir until the santen is dissolved. Reduce the heat and let the sauce simmer and thicken for about half an hour without a lid on, stirring occasionally. Serve the sauce with boiled eggs and garnish with leek, celery leaf and bawang goreng.

For the Kangkung katjang

Heat the oil in the wok and fry the onion, garlic and trassi bakar. Add the kangkung and stir-fry until it is al dente. Now add the salt and the sliced chilli pepper and let it cook for a few minutes while stirring.

To serve

Garnish the kangkung katjang with peanuts, and serve it with the sambal goreng telor and boiled rice.

Olive STORY

A name that evokes novelty and excitement could not be more fitting for Restaurant Elea, a dining experience in a little village that promises big flavour and plenty of surprises.

Restaurant Elea can be found between The Hague and Rotterdam in Rijswijk, combining the old with the brand new to create a completely individual style. Owners Bibi Kuyp and Takis Panagakis like to do things a little differently, an ethos reflected in everything from the name to the menus of their venture. Elea is the Ancient Greek word for olive, and was also once used by Greek philosophers to mean innovation, freedom, and challenge. Takis was born and raised in Greece, where he learned to cook, and still returns there yearly, always on the lookout for new ingredients to work with.

"Elea is a reflection of my origins and a nod to the future; a place to discover flavours and to be surprised. I want to share my knowledge, background and vision with our guests and let them experience something new."

An ambitious and award-winning chef known to many from his time working at Mazie in The Hague, Takis likes to look beyond the classic dishes. His team – Naomi van Es, his second in command, and Mike van der Weijden, his apprentice – help to produce the à la carte menu as well as the popular four to eight course menus, which almost everyone chooses despite each dish being an unknown according to Bibi, who hosts and manages the restaurant. The cooking style is "difficult to define," she says, "because Takis is always reinventing recipes, often using Greek ingredients or recipes but in unexpected ways."

His native country is a source of inspiration for all aspects of Restaurant Elea. Greek wines – expertly matched by the sommelier, Frank Stuyfzand – and other drinks accompany the dishes. Blue for beautiful Greek skies, the green of the olive trees, and the colour of sandy beaches transport the guests, and the warmth is reflected with the gold of the sun and the relaxed atmosphere that Elea is rich with. This is really important to Bibi, who leads by example in her small team. "Everybody has to be hands on and help each other," she explains, "and we want the guests to feel they can just be themselves here." Takis likes to speak to guests too, saying hello to each diner and getting feedback. Their aim in bringing a dream to life with Restaurant Elea is for the food to be unique, and for the care that goes into each detail to make each visit a lasting memory.

Restaurant Elea
SMOKED EEL WITH GREEK SALAD AND FETA ICE CREAM

At the restaurant, we serve this dish with oregano flowers, olive oil pearls, caper leaves, pitta croutons, and cucumber flowers, but you can decorate the salad in your own style.

Preparation time: 1 hour| Cooking time: 30 minutes| Serves: 4

Ingredients

For the Greek salad and gel:

12 cherry tomatoes

2 green peppers

6 mini cucumbers

40g pitted black Kalamata olives

2 shallots and 2 jalapeños

20ml olive oil

Salt, to taste

40g feta cheese

Pinch of oregano

4 leaves of gelatine

For the feta ice cream:

100ml cream

60ml milk

40g glucose

80g feta cheese

16g cortina

20g Pro Crema

For the black olive emulsion:

10ml white wine vinegar

100g yoghurt

50g egg white

20g pitted black Kalamata olives

50ml sunflower oil

To serve:

100g smoked eel

Method

For the Greek salad and gel

Set half of the tomatoes, green peppers, mini cucumbers, olives, shallots and jalapeños aside. Cut the remaining vegetables into thin round slices and arrange them in a circle on the plate. Drizzle half of the olive oil over the salad and sprinkle with salt.

To make the Greek salad gel, put the vegetables you set aside into a blender with the feta and oregano and blitz until everything is combined. Soak the gelatine in ice cold water. Sieve the pulp into a saucepan, and then gently warm 200g of the liquid. Add the gelatine and stir until it dissolves. Pour the mixture into a shallow tray and place in the fridge. When the mixture has set, cut out rounds to match the size of the vegetables in the salad and place them on the plate.

For the feta ice cream

Warm up the cream, milk and glucose to 80°c. Cool down and transfer the mixture into the blender with the remaining ingredients. Put in the ice cream machine and follow instructions to churn and chill until ready. If you don't have an ice cream maker, you can simply crumble the feta cheese over the Greek salad and gel.

For the black olive emulsion

Put all the ingredients into a blender or food processor and blend until just combined, then slowly add the oil little by little until it emulsifies.

To serve

Cut the smoked eel into pieces of the desired size and shape. Place them on the plate and then decorate the dish with dots of black olive emulsion and a neat scoop of the feta ice cream.

A world of DELICACIES

Gransjean Wijnen & Delicatessen is located in the beautiful Archipelbuurt area in The Hague, and specialises in the most delicious products from local producers as well as from all over the world.

Back in the 1920s, the shop that is now Gransjean Wijnen & Delicatessen started as a grocer's selling flour and sugar. Over the years it gained a reputation for the quality of its products, and today owner Jochem and his crew travel around the country and the world to continue searching out the finest products. For example, Gransjean has exclusive agreements with Acetaia Giuseppe Giusti, the world's oldest producer of balsamic vinegar, and Domaine de Barbe from Dordogne, a producer of fabulous pâté.

Of course, Holland is particularly famous for its cheeses, so Jochem is always looking for great farmhouse varieties, made by farmers with a vision and a story. Remeker and Nylander are two of the few farmers left who are producing cheese made from the raw milk of Jersey cows, without using antibiotics and only feeding their cows with natural products that grow on their own farms. Gransjean also works with de Zeekraal from the island of Terschelling, who focus on 100% biological sheep's cheese. The shop also offers the best quality cheese from abroad: Camembert, Epoisses de Bourgogne, Roquefort, the exquisite cheeses from cheesemaker Occelli (Piemond, Italy) and many more.

Jochem and his team are very proud of the diverse collection of cold cuts and cooked meats they have curated at Gransjean. Over 50 varieties line the shelves and counter, including 42-month-aged Pata Negra, Prosciutto di San Daniele, and Limousin Rosbeef to name just a few examples. The deli kitchen produces its own bread, makes fresh sandwiches and salads to take away, and creates a choice of six complete meals to take away in case you don't fancy cooking on a busy evening!

To accompany any meal, Gransjean has over 300 different wines to choose from. Next to big producers like Antinori, Barón de Ley, Miraval, MiP, Castello di Ama, Château Lynch Bages, Cloudy Bay, Moët & Chandon, Ruinart, Veuve Clicquot, and Dom Perignon, they have a range of wines from small farmers, working sustainably and all by hand, from all over the world. Burgundy, Bordeaux, Piemond, Chianti, Rioja, Marlborough, California, Mendoza, and more names signifying quality and the best flavours from every cuisine feature on the shelves; if you're looking for something special, you won't come away disappointed from this treasure trove on Bankastraat!

Gransjean Wijnen & Delicatessen

Gransjean Wijnen & Delicatessen

TRUFFLE RAVIOLI

This recipe is from an old friend from Piemond, Italy. He makes his own pasta and fills his own ravioli with truffle and ricotta. You can buy all of the ingredients below (except the fresh rocket) from us; Spiga al tartufo is the ravioli, which is filled with ricotta and truffle oil.

Preparation time: 15 minutes | Cooking time: approx. 15 minutes | Serves: 4

Ingredients

- 125g haricot verts
- 1kg spiga al tartufo
- 300ml cream
- 200g forest mushroom tapenade
- 100g crushed walnuts
- 250g Parmigiano Reggiano, grated
- 100g rocket
- A bottle of Riccardo Giusti balsamic vinegar (we recommend the 3* gold medal)

Method

Steam the haricot verts for 8 minutes. Cook the spiga al tartufo in a large pan of boiling water. They will only take 2 minutes. Mix the cream with the mushroom tapenade. Drain the spiga al tartufo and the haricot verts. Cut the haricot verts into three small pieces. Heat a pan and warm the spiga al tartufo, haricot verts, crushed walnuts and the creamy mushroom sauce together for 3 minutes.

If you want to add meat to this dish, bake a few slices of Prosciutto di San Daniele for just 1 minute on a tray in the oven, and then top the ravioli with them.

To serve

Serve the dish with grated Parmigiano Reggiano and rocket on top, dressed with a sprinkle of the balsamic. Don't forget to treat yourself with a fine glass of Barbaresco or Barolo too!

Wined and DINED

For directly imported wines from all over the world, tastings and stories from the producers, evening events and more, Marius Jouw Wijnvriend is the place to go in The Hague.

Marius began his career as a wine merchant in 2004 on a small scale, but with big ambitions. Having grown up in The Hague, the where of starting his own business had an obvious answer, but the how took a little more figuring out. The self-titled wine lover initially imported a small selection of international wines, drove to the city with the bottles in his car, and sold chilled rosé door to door! The following year he found a venue, though, and the first Marius Jouw Wijnvriend opened in 2005. Today, the business imports more than 800 wines directly from the producers, 25% of which are biological, and sells them to both wholesale and private customers across the city.

The team has grown too, from just Marius to a number of fellow wine enthusiasts with specialist roles. They all like to tell customers the stories behind the varieties they stock, as Marius tends towards working with small producers who are interesting, innovative or simply creating great wine. Sourcing might be dictated by the fairs and tastings he attends each year, as well as travelling to various vineyard-rich areas of Europe, where the majority of his wines come from, and samples of new vintages received at the shop, or

products discovered through other merchants in The Hague. Marius aims for the shop to be laid back and welcoming, so they always have lots of wines open to taste and plenty of expertise on hand for any customer.

Personable sales are what Marius emphasises at both The Hague and the second shop in Wassenaar, to set them apart from the many wine merchants out there. The kitchen at The Hague's shop is another unique feature, allowing Marius to collaborate with local restaurants for regular evening openings, featuring dinners cooked on the premises by a different restaurant's chefs each time, and wine flights to accompany the meal. The shop also hosts wine courses, for guests to learn about tasting and drinking, in partnership with WSET (the Wine & Spirit Education Trust).

From starting out with a love of wine and a fully stocked car, to running two award-winning shops and curating the Best Wine Assortment in the Netherlands three years in a row, Marius has certainly used his ambitions to their full potential. Marius Jouw Wijnvriend works to an ethos of delivering on what you promise in a way that's relaxed, reliable and most importantly, all about great wine.

Our wine PAIRINGS

Pairing wine and food can lead to glorious flavour combinations and unforgettable dinner parties. It can also turn out to be disastrous, leaving both cook and guests dissatisfied. There are countless ways of successfully matching food and wine though, many of which can be found on the internet, in cook books or by inquiring with your local foodie (or wine-geek). We have taken the liberty of listing some of our favourites here.

SPRECHEN VOUS ไทย

Alsace Gewürztraminer and Thai Chicken Curry

The region of Alsace has some identity issues. After having been tossed back and forth between Germany and France, and being the stage of many a conflict, it has ended up in French hands but its strong German influences are still noticeable. That being said, it should come as no surprise that the region is home to several grape varieties that have a slightly German ring to them, of which gewürztraminer is – without a doubt – the most instantly recognizable. It is highly aromatic, leaping from the glass and drowning the drinker in rosewater, perfume and sweet lychee juice. The in-your-face tropical fruit character allows the wine to be drunk with highly flavoursome dishes, and the small amount of residual sugar that the wine is bound to contain makes it an ideal partner for a spicy Asian curry. The German word for spice is Würze after all…

Domaine Fernand Engel Alsace gewürztraminer

VIVA AMERICANA

Chilean Carmenère and Chilli con (or sin) Carne

This combination is a game of two posers…both the dish and the wine like to pretend they are something they're not. OK, we may be exaggerating a little. But here's the story. The grape variety carmenère – today the national pride of wine-making Chile, but originally a Bordeaux varietal – has long been thought to be merlot. The first plantings in Chile date back to the mid-19th century, but it wasn't until 1998 that the cultivar was officially recognised as being carmenère. Then there is chilli con carne; a dish often believed to be Mexican, actually a Texan classic. Fair enough, the two share a border, so mutual influences are likely to happen, but still. So let's join chilli and Chile in a combination that's rich, velvety and has a spicy kick in both the food and the wine.

Viña Falernia Elqui carmenère

Marius Jouw Wijnvriend

'I'M NOT DRINKING ANY MERLOT!'

New Zealand Pinot Noir and Tuna Tataki

Merlot: the world's most accessible red wine. And the most boring, if we are to believe Miles Raymond on his wine-fuelled road trip in the film Sideways. So instead, let's talk about the varietal that shines in the same picture, and that is celebrated for yielding some of the globe's most beguiling and precious wines: pinot noir. A notoriously hard grape to grow – susceptible to pretty much every disease and fungus in the book – but when it's well made, it's fresh but silky, precise but complex, sweet but savoury; any wine lover's dream. So much so that we recommend travelling 18,500 kilometres from The Hague to Marlborough, New Zealand, to try a wine that offers everything that makes pinot noir such a joy to drink. If you have the time, pop by your local fishmonger on the way back and get a fresh tuna steak or two (not bluefin). Give it a quick sear, give the wine a quick chill, and you'll smiling from ear to ear. Look up tuna tataki for a more elaborate preparation.

Clos Marguerite Marlborough pinot noir.

WHITE PEPPER & WHITE GOLD

Austrian Grüner Veltliner and White Asparagus

Grüner veltliner, or simply grüner, as it is sometimes called, is the most widely planted grape variety in Austria and is responsible for some of the best white wines the alpine country has to offer. Styles range from fresh and simple to complex and age-worthy, but an aroma that is often heard in tasting notes with this varietal is that of white pepper. Now, we don't expect you to jump up from your chair in excitement when you hear that. So, luckily, the wines may also display an array of citrus and stone fruit aromas, and can even develop a honey-like richness with years of bottle-ageing. It is the richer style that lends itself perfectly to combine with the pride of Holland's only semi-mountainous (read: hilly) region: white asparagus from Limburg. Beautiful as a lowland classic with eggs, butter and ham, but if you're not bound to tradition, feel free to grill or stir-fry the Dutch white gold to build on the crisp, fresh, and peppery notes in the wine.

Weingut Huber Traisental grüner veltliner "Obere Steigen"

LE PLAT DU JOUR

Loire Cabernet Franc and Steak Tartare

Walk into a Parisian bistro on any given day and you'll be sure to find steak tartare on the menu; that is, raw beef, finely cut up and served with several possible types of garnish (including a raw egg yolk). Not surprisingly, this is a dish that has as many enemies as it has enthusiasts. The wine list in said bistro is bound to offer a cabernet franc from the Loire, probably by the glass. These wines can count on a similar mix of lovers and haters among the wine-drinking public. So you could say this classical French bistro pair is a marriage of misunderstood anti-heroes, driven into each other's arms by the mean carnivorous/alcoholic public. Less romantically put, it is a wonderful combination of pure, clean flavours, with a savoury character that the wine and dish share. If you like cooking – well, cutting really – this is a fun dish to prepare at home. Be sure to get a fresh cut of meat from your local butcher, and throw in several condiments and garnishes to spice it up. Finally, do not forget to put your wine in the fridge for 15 minutes before serving to lift its fresh, fruity character.

Fréderic Mabileau St. Nicolas de Bourgueil cabernet franc

WORTH THE EXTRA DENTAL CARE

Montilla-Moriles Pedro Ximénez and Chocolate Pecan Pie

To those looking for a serious sugar rush, the combination of sweet chocolate pecan pie and the treacly goodness that is pedro ximénez may well be the holy grail of food and wine pairings. The grapes for this wine are put to dry on mats under the merciless Andalusian sun – a process called asoleo – leaving them in a raisin-like state with a sky-high sugar to juice ratio. Now imagine those raisins pressed, vinified, fortified and aged in oak barrels (solera)… oh, the sweetness! Fortunately, well-made pedro ximénez matches this sugar-rich character with intense aromas of various dried fruits, maple syrup, roasted nuts, coffee and even chocolate. As our mouths begin to water, we are left with no other choice than to book a preliminary dental appointment and go for the double-trouble-chocolate-combo. Don't feel guilty, nuts are healthy.

Alvear Montilla-Moriles pedro ximénez 1927

Legendary THAI

Bright fresh flavours are at the heart of Restaurant Naga Thai, combining traditional recipes with innovative twists to showcase the best of Thai gastronomy.

Since opening in 2009, Restaurant Naga Thai has opened its doors to the Den Haag community as one of the city's multiple eateries contributing towards a rich and vibrant Asian culinary scene. Named after the Legend of the Naga (a supernatural being in the shape of a serpent or dragon believed to have birthed the Mekong) the restaurant has been busy carving out its own legend by providing the best quality food cooked from the freshest and most authentic ingredients.

In addition to the restaurant's Thai staff, Naga Thai's traditional feel and taste is brought to life by head chef Mit Mungruayklang who discovered his love for cooking at a young age in his small village in North-Eastern Thailand. With the influence of his own family's cooking along with skills gained throughout his time at Bangkok's renowned Busaracum Restaurant, Mit describes Naga Thai's menu as a mix of traditional cuisine combined with a contemporary 'wow feature' that gives the restaurant its signature style. The meals created in Naga Thai's kitchen incorporate a variety of techniques and complex balancing of flavours that are the cornerstone of traditional Thai cooking. Through an intricate play of hot, sour, sweet, salty, and bitter elements, Naga Thai puts its own unique stamp on classics such as Tom Yum soup, a particular favourite.

This hybrid of old classics with new twists is reflected in the buzzing atmosphere and contemporary interior at Naga Thai, where customers can enjoy personable service amidst the restaurant's gold and wooden themed décor in a modern, bright and open space. Located in the heart of the city's Statenkwartier quarter, it also boasts an open terrace to watch the hustle and bustle of the famous Frederik Hendriklaan shopping street. From the aroma of fresh home cooking when you walk in, to the smiling Buddha statue, Naga Thai channels the vibrant energy and culture of Thailand together with Den Haag's flare for culinary innovation to create a restaurant worthy of its own legend.

Naga Thai
GREEN PAPAYA SALAD

This recipe was adapted from an ethnic Lao dish known as 'Tam Som' which used local fruits and vegetables such as green (unripe) mango or papaya as the main ingredient. The dish combines the five main tastes of the local cuisine: sour lime, hot chilli, salty savoury fish sauce and sweetness added by palm sugar. A Thai salad can be cool, refreshing and pungent, all at once.

Preparation time: 30 minutes | Cooking time: 15 minutes | Serves: 2

Ingredients

1 green papaya

2-3 yard long beans (also called asparagus or snake beans), cut into 2cm lengths

3 cloves of garlic

2 fresh red bird's eye chillies, deseeded and sliced

2 fresh green bird's eye chillies, deseeded and sliced

8-10 cherry tomatoes, halved

1 tbsp finely chopped dried shrimp

2 tbsp crushed roasted peanuts

For the dressing:

¼ cup (60ml) lime juice

2 tbsp Thai fish sauce

1 tbsp grated palm sugar

1 tbsp superfine sugar

Method

Cut the papaya in half lengthways. Scrape out the seeds with a spoon and discard, and then shred the papaya coarsely. Boil the yard long beans for 2-3 minutes in a large pan of water until tender. Drain, rinse under cold water and drain again.

Put the garlic and bird's eye chillies in a large mortar and grind to a paste with a pestle. Add the shredded papaya, a small amount at a time, pounding with a pestle until it becomes slightly soft. Add the yard long bean, cherry tomatoes and dried shrimp to the mortar and crush them lightly with the pestle until they are incorporated.

Whisk the ingredients for the dressing until combined, and then add it to the salad in the mortar. Toss gently to combine.

To serve

Transfer the salad to a serving dish and sprinkle with the crushed roasted peanuts.

Seafood and EAT IT!

All the style and sophistication of a restaurant on the beach, with beautifully presented fish and seafood dishes accompanied by good wine, and an atmosphere to relax and indulge in.

Owners Preshaan and Leonard set up Oceans Beach House because Preshaan loves seafood and they both love the beach! The two met while working at a restaurant in The Hague, became good friends, and ten years ago decided to start their own business in the hospitality industry they both wanted to continue being part of. Their restaurant is one of four the pair now own and run in Scheveningen, and has a top spot on the Strandweg Boulevard with a beautiful outlook over sea and sand.

In the midst of many casual eateries and bars on the boulevard, Oceans is an oasis of luxurious food, wine, and professional service with an emphasis on presentation in every aspect of the restaurant. The menu focuses on seafood and fish dishes; from lobster to oysters and caviar to sashimi, the offering is all about the freshest produce, sourced from Schmidt – the famous Dutch fishing company – and delivered straight to the kitchen to then be impeccably prepared by experienced chefs. The team know and work together well, having moved between Preshaan and Leonard's restaurants to hone their skills and bring the high standards of the business with them.

The menu has recently evolved to offer more options for those with different dietary requirements too, such as gluten-free and vegan; a popular addition has been the Hawaiian poké bowls which are filled with sushi rice, delicate pieces of raw fish and zingy toppings and have been really well received by all. It's important to the owners that Oceans stands out for its smart, stylish, and upmarket approach to dining at the beach. That's not to say they don't want guests to feel totally relaxed, however, so the friendly front of house team will make sure everyone feels welcome. Some gentle jazz in the background and a generous list of wine and bubbly usually helps as well!

Developing their restaurants to keep things moving forward is a key part of Preshaan and Leonard's success. At Oceans, ideas are always shared between experienced and younger members of staff to allow room for innovation and improvement; young managers Jaqueline and Aissa bring their enthusiasm and commitment to the existing style and sophistication of Oceans Beach House. It's a collaboration between the best ingredients Scheveningen can provide: beachside dining, unbeatably fresh fish and seafood, and a love of great hospitality from both hosts and diners.

Oceans Beach House
FRUITS DE MER

Preshaan loves to eat Fruits de Mer, so he thought that a variety of raw and cooked shellfish served as a chilled platter would be a great dish to enjoy at the beach house with the ocean view. We source our seafood from Schmidt Zeevis in Rotterdam, which has the best quality and freshest catch.

Preparation time: 30 minutes | Cooking time: 20 minutes | Serves: 2

Ingredients

2 Bretagne oysters

2 Normandy oysters

1 lobster

50g cockles

50g clams

Ensis
(a variety of edible saltwater clam)

1 sprig of rosemary

2 sprigs of chervil

1 tbsp tomato purée

50ml white wine

1 clove of garlic, crushed

50g Dutch shrimp

30g prawns

50g Icelandic shrimp

30g pandalus borealis
(a variety of shrimp)

Splash of white wine

1 tsp paprika

2 crab claws

To serve:

Crushed ice

Dash of Tabasco sauce

50ml red wine vinaigrette

2 lemons

Butter, melted

1 tsp paprika

Method

Firstly, open both the Bretagne and Normandy oysters. Place the lobster into boiling water with a little salt and cook for 8 minutes. When done, take it out of the water and place in the fridge to cool for 10 minutes. Put all the shellfish (the cockles, clams and ensis) into a large stainless steel pan, then add the rosemary, chervil, tomato purée, wine and garlic. Cover with a lid or tin foil and leave to steam for 6 minutes in the oven at 180°c. Cook all the shrimp and prawns in a pan on a medium heat with a splash of white wine and paprika for 2 minutes. The crab claws don't need any cooking and are served in the shell.

To serve

Take a large round plate or platter and cover it with crushed ice. Using large flat seashells, separate each type of shellfish and crustacean to present them in the seashells on top of the crushed ice. Serve the oysters with Tabasco, red wine vinaigrette and wedges of lemon on the side. Cut the chilled lobster in half down the centre from head to tail, and dress with melted butter mixed with a pinch of paprika. French fries and cooked vegetables work well as side dishes.

Sunshine and SUSHI

2017 saw the arrival of Hawaiian cuisine for The Hague in the form of Ohana Poké, a restaurant serving up bowls of goodness, chilled vibes, and authentic flavours fresh from island shores.

Ohana Poké opened in September 2017 as the brainchild of Kok Yong Khaw and his friend, chef Berry Le. Having worked in a sushi restaurant together, they decided that the time was right to bring something unique to The Hague's food scene. Using a basis of fresh fish and exciting approaches to healthy eating, the pair researched various countries for undiscovered culinary concepts and hit on Hawaiian food. They put a menu together with a focus on food that's easy to prepare, fun to eat, not too expensive, and really tasty! Kok Yong designed the clean, minimalist restaurant in the city centre which opens for casual lunches and early dinners, allowing people to enjoy a relaxed dining experience that has grown and grown in popularity.

If you haven't heard of poké already, then Ohana Poké is ready and waiting to introduce the Hawaiian dish in all its glory. Traditionally, poké is a fish salad that is freshly caught, diced, seasoned and ready to serve. Ohana's Poké Bowl is a new approach to this concept, and contains a base of rice or salad topped with fresh vegetables, fruits, proteins, garnishes and sprinkles. Berry's kitchen team use sushi rice they mix themselves, as well as fish from sustainable suppliers in Amsterdam and Scheveningen and a whole variety of organic vegetables bought in daily from local farmers. The idea is for diners to customise their own bowl, though the menu does provide a few tried and tested 'signature' combinations that can be ordered as a bowl or a sushurrito – that's sushi in a burrito – or the more traditional Japanese nori roll.

Fresh ingredients are not the only order of the day at Ohana, as Kok Yong also wanted to create a relaxed space to hang out and eat food that's prepared fast, with flavour and health as his top priorities. The final key element is the family who run it together, comprised of Kok Yong and Berry, Kok Yong's sister, and their 'crew'. As Berry says, "I'm one of the owners, but it doesn't feel like that, because we are all equal and like family to each other here."

Ohana Poké

Ohana Poké
THE ALOHA WAY

This dish is one of our all-time favourites at Ohana Poké.
Fresh salmon, sushi rice, and a lot of fresh veggies. Try it out yourself
and see why it's our favourite!

Preparation time: 15 minutes | Cooking time: 20 minutes | Serves: 2

Ingredients

For the base:

250g white sushi rice

3 tbsp rice vinegar

2 tsp sugar

1 tsp salt

For the marinade:

4 tbsp sesame oil

2 tbsp soy sauce

½ tsp grated fresh ginger

½ tsp white sesame seeds, lightly toasted

½ tsp black sesame seeds, lightly toasted

Pinch of sugar

For the toppings:

250g sashimi grade salmon, cut into 1cm cubes

200g cucumber, cut into 1cm cubes

150g edamame beans (soy beans)

1 avocado, peeled and sliced

150g orange masago

For the finishing touches:

Kewpie Japanese mayonnaise

½ tsp white sesame seeds, lightly toasted

½ tsp black sesame seeds, lightly toasted

Seaweed flakes (nori)

Soy sauce

Method

For the base

To cook the rice, place the rice in a saucepan with a close-fitting lid. Cover the rice with cold water and, using your hand, stir gently to release the excess starch from the grains. Drain and repeat until the water stops turning cloudy. Soak the rice and leave it aside for 20 minutes; this will give the rice a better texture when cooked.

Cover the rice with the following amount of cold water: 240ml for white, 360ml for brown. Place the saucepan on a medium-high heat and bring to a rapid boil. Cover, turn down the heat to a gentle simmer, and cook for the following length of time: 15-20 minutes for white, 20 minutes for brown.

Once the rice is cooked, remove the pan from the heat and leave, covered, to steam for a further 10 minutes. Now you can turn the rice out into a wooden sushi rice bowl, if you have one. Using a rice paddle or wooden spoon, gently fold and turn the cooked rice, allowing the steam to evaporate. At this stage, we like to season the freshly cooked rice. Whisk the rice wine vinegar with the sugar and salt, then drizzle the mixture over the hot rice while gently folding to coat each grain. The rice should now be left for 15 minutes to cool before using for your poké bowl.

For the marinade

Combine all the ingredients for the marinade in a small bowl and then add the salmon to it and stir gently to cover the fish. Set aside for 10 minutes.

For the toppings and finishing touches

Now we can start assembling the bowl. Divide the rice between two serving bowls and put the cucumber, edamame beans, avocado, fish and masago on top in any order you like. Then it's time to finish it off with some Japanese mayonnaise, followed by sprinkling over the sesame seeds and cut seaweed. Do use some soy sauce, if you like it, in your bowl. Now your poké is ready and dinner is served! Enjoy.

A new ERA

The Roeleveld family have brought a touch of French flair to Den Haag with their make-over of a community favourite.

During the height of its popularity, the former Old Jazz Café existed at the heart and soul of its neighbourhood. An iconic place known for its homey atmosphere where many good memories were made, the Old Jazz was the quintessence of the Netherlands' celebrated Brown Café culture. Brown cafés are casual neighbourhood gathering spots located all across the country where patrons can enjoy regional food and local beers. After a lull in popularity, the Roeleveld family saw the opportunity to rescue the Old Jazz, giving it a second life as an exciting and relevant part of the community.

With the full refurbishment of its interior, the Old Jazz has been opened up into a bright and inviting space, breathing a new life and style of dining into the café. It now sports a sophisticated French character with mirrored walls and a black and green interior. An emphasis on local produce as well as an international mix of meat and fish dishes and wines from across the globe informs the menu, and behind the brass and marble bar one of the chefs does live cooking. The sushi and flamkuchen are made on show here so customers can watch their food being prepared. The café's broad menu reflects its contemporary international feel and is made to the same high standard the Roeleveld family puts into everything they do.

Right next door to the Seafoodbar Vigo, the Old Jazz exists independently from the restaurant while serving as the perfect place to enjoy an aperitif or retire for a drink after your seafood indulgence, generating a sense of community along the Aert van der Goesstraat. Despite its contemporary style and interior, the focus on keeping the bar's feeling of 'gezellig' was an important part of bringing the Old Jazz into the new era. While gezellig literally translates into English as 'cosy', the true sentiment behind the Dutch word has no exact English equivalent. A word that encompasses Den Haag's culture, gezellig describes time spent with loved ones, seeing a friend after a long absence, or just general togetherness. True to their family orientation, the Old Jazz is another example of the Roeleveld family's passion for hospitality, where they have succeeded in combining the height of quality food and service with the feeling of gezellig that seems to follow wherever they go.

THE OLD
JAZZ

DRINKS & DINNER

The Old Jazz
BEEF TATAKI

Tataki is an original Japanese dish that can be made with fish or meat, which is always raw inside and lightly grilled outside. It was invented by Sakomoto Ryoma around 200 years ago. In our version, we use beef sirloin because it's really tender.

Preparation time: 15 minutes, plus 30 minutes or overnight
Cooking time: approx. 10 minutes | Serves: 4 as a starter

Ingredients

400g sirloin

100ml Korean bulgogi sauce

For the sweet and sour cucumber:

1 cucumber

60ml vinegar

40g sugar

Pinch of black pepper

For the enoki and garlic crisps:

Tempura flour

Sparkling water

Large pinch of curry powder

200g enoki

1 clove of garlic

For the curry mayonnaise:

1 tsp curry powder

2 egg yolks

15ml white wine vinegar

300ml peanut oil

To finish:

100g wakame (seaweed salad)

Method

Cut the beef into long strips around 5cm wide. Put a pan on a high heat with a little bit of oil. Scorch the beef for a very short amount of time on each side. Set aside to rest. Put the bulgogi sauce in a pan and cook until it has reduced and is thick. Glaze the beef with the thick bulgogi sauce and then cut the beef into very thin slices.

For the sweet and sour cucumber

Put 120ml of water into a bowl with the vinegar, sugar and black pepper. Cut the cucumber into four pieces and discard the seeded parts. Cut the rest of the cucumber finely and put it in the bowl with the other ingredients. Let it rest for at least 30 minutes; we prefer to leave it overnight so the flavour develops. You only need a quarter of the pickled cucumber for this dish.

For the enoki and garlic crisps

Mix enough tempura flour and sparkling water, adding a bit of each gradually, to get a thin, smooth batter. Add a large pinch of curry powder and then stir through the enoki until well coated. Deep fry the mushrooms at 180°c until golden brown. Slice the garlic very thinly (we prefer to do it on a mandoline) and fry until just golden.

For the curry mayonnaise

Cook out the curry powder in a pan, and then cool down. Put the egg yolks, the curry powder and white wine vinegar in the food processor. Turn the processor on and very slowly and gradually add the peanut oil with the machine running. Be careful that it doesn't split, otherwise you will need to start again. Keep the food processor running until you have a smooth mayonnaise.

To finish

Put 100g of beef on each plate, and dress with some wakame, sweet and sour cucumber, crispy enoki and fried garlic. Add drops of the curry mayonnaise around the outside and it's ready to serve. Eet smakelijk!

Harvesting GOODNESS

Focused on natural, fresh ingredients and modern French cuisine with Dutch influences, Restaurant Oogst turns bountiful harvests into seasonal feasts.

Restaurant Oogst is co-owned by Alexander Spanakis and Marcel van der Kleijn, who established it in 2015 following his other ventures in The Hague, Restaurant Calla's and BIT Grill & Café. Alexander is front of house at Oogst, and is just as passionate about his role in the restaurant now as he was when it opened. He and Crysta curate the relaxed atmosphere that showcases chefs' Emma and Brandt's creativity in the kitchen; they are all encouraged to put their personality into the cooking, plating and serving of the food, which is described as modern French cuisine with Dutch influences.

The young venture is already known for its dishes blooming with local produce, especially seasonal fare from Laantje Voorham. This garden in Wassenaar, named after Arie Voorham who began a collaboration with Marcel a few years ago and now cultivates rare edible crops, has a microclimate that makes it possible to grow many varieties of herbs, flowers, salads and vegetables which are used at both Calla's and Oogst. A unique set up, it enables the menus at Oogst to be refreshed every five to six weeks according to the latest harvest – which is the meaning of the restaurant's name – which is picked by the chefs every two or three days.

True to this ethos, summer menus are vibrant whereas winter menus tend towards the more sober, simple meals that satisfy the craving for comfort over colder months. Guests can choose whether they want to be 'completely taken care of' with an aperitif, savoury and sweet dishes, matching wines and hot drinks, or enjoy a three to five course meal from the current selection of dishes and wines. Alexander and the team want Restaurant Oogst to be accessible and welcoming to all ages, with no pretences about their style of dining.

"We really try to welcome people and make them feel at ease," says Alexander, an aim which is reflected in the intimate, cosy but classy interior of the dining room. The restaurant only seats a few people at tables of two amidst classical Baroque décor, and this refined space creates a real experience when paired with the eating and drinking. At Restaurant Oogst, a genuine interest in seasonal, exciting, naturally delicious food and drink is the order of the day, and the small venture continues to blossom thanks to its team's love for what they do.

Restaurant Oogst
BURRATA CHEESE AND TOMATO SALAD WITH SAN MARZANO BROTH

This dish truly represents our conceptual thinking when designing a seasonal menu. It was created by our chefs for our summer menu in 2016. Tomatoes are at their best around June; juicy, full of flavours and vitamins. We like serving ingredients as fresh as possible and showcasing their raw value. Putting a salad together sounds easy, but achieving a perfect blend of flavours and structures with minimum processing of ingredients is more complicated than you would think!

Preparation time: 30 minutes, plus overnight for the broth | Serves: 4

Ingredients

For the broth:

1kg San Marzano ripe tomatoes

1 red onion

2 cloves of garlic

2 tbsp salt

1 tsp pepper

15 basil leaves

2g xantana (xanthan gum)

For the salad:

1 coeur de boeuf tomato

2 green zebra tomatoes

12 yellow pear tomatoes

150g cherry tomatoes

2 burrata cheeses

Extra-virgin olive oil

White pepper

A few sprigs of fresh basil

Tomato powder (preferably homemade, which you can do by drying tomato skins in the oven and then grating them)

1 tsp balsamic vinegar

Method

The transparent broth of San Marzano tomatoes needs to be prepared the day before.

Put all the ingredients for the broth, except the xantana, in a blender or food processor to combine. After 4 minutes of blending/processing, put the mixture in a wet strainer cloth in a sieve, ideally a conical one, over a bowl. Turn the corners of the cloth clockwise to increase the pressure. Let the liquid drain out for 24 hours at room temperature. The next day, put the transparent San Marzano juice in a clean bowl and mix it with the xantana until it becomes a velvety broth. Add more salt and pepper if necessary after tasting.

For the salad

Wash all the tomatoes with cold water and let them dry. Cut four horizontal slices from the coeur de boeuf. Cut off the top of the green zebras and extract the core with a spoon. Peel half of the cherry tomatoes by carefully cutting a cross in the bottom of each tomato. Put them in boiling water for 10 seconds, and then peel the skin from the bottom towards the top but don't remove it.

To serve

Use bright white plates, or ones with a colourful design. Pour two or three tablespoons of broth into the middle of the plate first, and lay one big slice of the coeur de boeuf on top. Cut the burrata cheese in half and put one part on the tomato, with the cut side facing up. Pour some olive oil over the cheese and season with white pepper. Divide the remaining tomatoes over the dishes (some cut and some whole). Place one of the green zebra tomato cores on each plate.

Garnish the salad with some basil leaves, using a mixture of smaller and bigger ones. Try to turn some inside out for a nice detailed effect. Top the salad off with some tomato powder. Just seconds before serving (otherwise it will dilute in the broth) add a few dashes of balsamic vinegar over the salad, and then enjoy.

Macaron
MAGIC

With a passion for authentic French pastries and desserts, Patisserie Jarreau offers every flavour of macaron and the workshops to make them yourself.

There are two kinds of people in this world; those who love French patisseries, and those who are yet to visit Patisserie Jarreau. Since the shop's opening, the residents of Den Haag have enjoyed the French patisserie's freshly baked pastries and handmade sweets for almost 30 years. Created by partners Roel and Jaqueline, the name 'Jarreau' is a clever French take on the fusion of both their names, each giving a piece of themselves to the title and soul of the patisserie.

Located just outside central Den Haag in the historic Benoordenhout quarter, visitors of the patisserie often begin as curious window shoppers caught by the store's striking window display. Once inside, the interior of Jarreau boasts big and beautiful glass cabinets brimming with colourful creations for you to take home or enjoy in the park right on the store's front doorstep. Designed for takeaway, Roel and Jaqueline say they've kept the patisserie small to intensify their focus on the food itself and to better deliver the high quality they've come to be known for. After landing third place at the world competitions in Stuttgart and being awarded Patisserie of the Year in 2007, Jarreau is a regular pit-stop for sweet-toothed locals as well as an attraction for tourists.

Proving that one visit is never enough, customers of Jarreau often revisit the patisserie for their timeless favourites such as the salted caramel macarons or chocolate bonbons, or to try something completely new from their ever-changing seasonal creations. While Roel and Jaqueline offer an extensive variety of pastries, chocolates, tarts and friands made from scratch and with the best locally sourced ingredients, it's their macarons that really steal the show. Because of this, workshops are offered for those who want to be part of the whole magical process. Taught by Roel himself and others in Jarreau's team of skilled patissiers, the workshops offer step-by-step sessions that allow you to truly master the delicate treat, notorious for being tricky to make but well worth the effort. Patisserie Jarreau has won the hearts of locals and tourists alike, earning its reputation as the place to go for a little piece of France in the centre of Den Haag.

JARREAU   PÂTISSERIE | CHOCOLATERIE

MACARONS • MACARONS • MACARONS • MACARONS • MACARONS

Patisserie Jarreau
SALTED CARAMEL MACARONS

French macarons are composed of almond flour, icing sugar and egg whites. Tant-pour-tant is an expression referring to the equal parts of almond flour and icing sugar. 'Macaronage' is the stage in preparing French macaron shells where the batter is worked until it's smooth, shiny and flowing, which is essential to the process.

Preparation time: 2 hours | Cooking time: 15–20 minutes | Makes: 50

Ingredients

For the macaron shells:

252g ground almonds

252g icing sugar

252g granulated sugar

63ml water

92g egg whites

3g ochre yellow food colouring

92g egg whites

A few ice cream cones, crushed

For the filling:

160g cream

10g glucose syrup

35g butter

85g granulated sugar

2g salt

115g milk chocolate (35%)

Method

For the batter

Mix the ground almonds and icing sugar together in the food processor and then sieve the mixture to get a fine powder (tant-pour-tant). Boil the granulated sugar and water until the mixture reaches 115°c. Begin to whisk the egg whites at this point. Meanwhile, continue to boil the syrup until it reaches 118°c, and then pour it gently into the frothy egg whites with the mixer still on. Whisk at half speed until the mixture is approximately 45°c.

Meanwhile, mix the tant-pour-tant, food colouring and the non-whisked egg whites together in a bowl. Add the frothy egg white and sugar mixture in two parts and continue to whisk after each addition until the batter has a glossy shine (macaronage). Fill a piping bag with batter and pipe out into even-sized rounds on a tray lined with a silicone mat or baking paper. Gently tap the tray on the counter to smooth out the surface of your macaron shells. Sprinkle with the crushed cones for decoration and then leave the shells to form a crust for 30 minutes. Bake the macarons in a preheated oven for 15-20 minutes at 150°c and then leave to cool on the tray, out of the oven.

For the filling

Heat the cream, glucose syrup and butter to 80°c. Caramelise the granulated sugar in a separate pan, and then once the caramel is the desired colour, stir in the warmed cream mixture over a low heat until the sugar is completely melted (beware of splashing!). Add the salt and then pour the liquid on to the chocolate. Whisk until the mixture has a glossy shine. Transfer the filling to a clean bowl, cover with foil and chill in the fridge for about 2 hours.

To serve

Once cooled, fill the macaron shells with the set salted caramel and then chill in the fridge for 12 hours to obtain the best 'bite'. Serve at room temperature.

Artistic LICENCE

New, innovative and internationally influenced – Portfolio is a restaurant
that aims to excite and please diners with a balanced approach
to flavour and eating out.

After ten years of working together in the restaurant industry, Remco and his business partner Kasper set up their own venture in The Hague, their home city. They were looking for something new to fill a gap they spotted and decided to combine their experiences, bringing everything they had learnt together to create a dining experience that would be personal, exciting and different. Portfolio opened in November 2017 with Kasper as head chef and Remco as front of house manager and sommelier.

They describe the food at Portfolio as "modern, with influences from all over the world featuring in the dishes," with a focus on natural produce and wines that aim to surprise and delight with bold flavours and elegant style. The restaurant's food offering comprises one set menu, which changes as frequently as new ideas come to the team. Authenticity is a big part of the Portfolio ethos; if they're riffing on Asian cuisine then those influences should come through clearly when the diner tastes the dish.

There's no intention to hide away in the food or otherwise at Portfolio; with a kitchen right in the middle of the open plan space everything is on show, and the tight-knit team – usually just four people – must work seamlessly together as part of the dining experience. The space is intimate too, and has a combination of low tables and stools along the bar which Remco finds important to create dynamism in the restaurant. During the day and evening, returning guests have shown just how popular the venture has already been with bookings far in advance.

"The most important thing for us is to keep guests excited and happy," says Remco. He and Kasper try to achieve this not only with an ever-evolving menu that even regular diners won't have seen before, but with personal and friendly service too. Kasper and his sous chef will sometimes come to the table with a meal, and the maître d' and Remco enjoy being on familiar terms with guests. It's an experience that is still changing as the restaurant grows; the owners like to experiment and have embraced the freedom their own place has given them to work on a basis of continual improvement and becoming an exciting new addition to The Hague's culinary innovators.

Portfolio
HAMACHI CEVICHE

To make this dish even quicker to make, you can buy ready-made kimchi, and use sushi ginger instead of making the ginger gel yourself.

Preparation time: 2 hours, plus 2 days marinating | Serves: 8

Ingredients

For the watermelon kimchi:

300g water

15g sugar

22g salt

20g spring onion

12g ginger

5g garlic

3g dried shrimps

2g chilli pepper

150g white watermelon (the part between the flesh and the skin)

For the ginger gel:

775ml water

300g sugar

375ml lime juice

200g ginger

16g agar agar

16g gellan

For the Hamachi marinade:

1 cucumber

200g cherry tomatoes

1 bundle of celery

½ bunch of coriander

5 limes, juiced

400g Hamachi (or a different fish like sea bass or dorade)

For the avocado crème:

2 avocados

Splash of sushi vinegar

Pinch of salt and white pepper

For the vinaigrette:

75ml Hamachi marinade

75ml lime or lemon oil

To serve:

1 or 2 kumquats

Aji amarillo (you can also use jalapeños)

Method

For the watermelon kimchi

Boil the water, then dissolve the sugar and salt in it and let it cool. Finely chop all the other ingredients except the watermelon and add to the water mixture. Grate the watermelon on a mandoline and add it to the marinade. Leave to marinate in the fridge for two days.

For the ginger gel

Mix all the ingredients apart from the agar agar and gellan together in a pan and bring to the boil. Purée everything with a hand mixer and then push the purée through a fine sieve. Bring the mixture to the boil again with all of the agar agar and gellan. Leave it to cool down and set in the fridge, then blend together in a food processor or blender until it becomes a smooth gel.

For the Hamachi marinade

Put all of the ingredients into a blender, then pass through a fine sieve. Marinate the Hamachi for 20 minutes in the marinade.

For the avocado crème

Clean the avocados and put the flesh into a blender. Blend until it becomes a smooth crème, and then add sushi vinegar, salt and pepper to taste.

For the vinaigrette

Combine the ceviche marinade with the lime or lemon oil.

To serve

Put one tablespoon of avocado crème onto a plate. Place the kimchi onto the plate, then add the marinated fish, followed by the ginger gel, kumquat slices and aji amarillo or jalapeño slices. Before serving, add some of the marinade around the dish.

Heart and SOLE

The Roeleveld family have combined their passion for excellent service and fresh fish in Den Haag's seafood sensation, Seafoodbar Vigo.

All over the world, there are some associations we can never separate: when you think of Burgundy you think wine, when you think of Belgium you think chocolate, and for those who call Den Haag home, fish is the first thing that springs to mind when thinking of Seafoodbar Vigo. The restaurant is located on the Aert van der Goesstraat in Scheveningen, one of the city's most northern districts known for its long sandy beaches and flourishing seafood industry. Scheveningen is home to both of the Roeleveld family's latest restaurant ventures, Seafoodbar Vigo and its little sister Vigo Cantina, as well as the recently purchased Old Jazz Café only one door down.

Seafoodbar Vigo is supplied by the Roeleveld's fishing business, meaning that the fish are bought directly from the fishermen and prepared the same evening by Vigo's chefs. The period of time between catch to table is therefore as short as it can be, and this hands-on approach allows Vigo to serve only the freshest and finest quality fish to customers. With an extensive continental wine list boasting the best of Spanish, Italian, French and Portuguese vintages, Vigo has plenty to pair with seasonal catches and customer favourites. One such favourite is the halibut dish, incorporating the saltiness of the sea, the earthy flavours of the shiitake mushrooms and the fresh hit of the miso lime beurre blanc.

The restaurant's open layout, natural lighting and upbeat atmosphere gives customers a taste of what's to come as soon as they walk in to Vigo. Best described as gezellig, which literally translates into English as 'cosy', Vigo is an example of this Dutch sentiment that can mean time spent with loved ones, seeing a friend after a long absence, or just general togetherness. True to their ethos, Vigo is a perfect example of the Roeleveld family's passion for great hospitality, where they have succeeded in combining the height of quality food and service with the feeling of gezellig. Whether it's for the restaurant's relaxed atmosphere or the menu filled with the finest fish Den Haag has to offer, the Seafoodbar Vigo is a must visit for any resident or visitor.

Seafoodbar Vigo
HALIBUT WITH SWEET POTATO CREAM

This halibut dish is one of the favourites from the Vigo menu. It has everything: the saltiness of the sea aster, the earthy flavours of the shiitake, and of course the fresh and flavourful miso and lime beurre blanc, in combination with one of the most delicious fishes. Like we say, geniet er van!

Preparation time: 20 minutes | Cooking time: approx. 1 hour | Serves: 4

Ingredients

To make your own fish stock:

500g fish bones

1 carrot, leek, onion and stick of celery, all finely chopped

1 bay leaf

1 tsp whole black peppercorns

Dash of white wine

For the sweet potato cream:

1 big sweet potato

100ml cream

50g butter

For the miso and lime beurre blanc:

500ml fish stock

500ml cream

100g butter

2 tsp miso paste

1 lime

For the halibut:

Knob of butter, clarified

4 200g halibut fillets

For the garnish:

500g shiitake, chopped

500g sea aster

10ml chicken stock

Salt and pepper

Method

To make your own fish stock

Put all the ingredients into a big pan with two litres of cold water. Boil for 30 minutes while skimming off the foam. Strain the stock through a cloth to finish.

For the sweet potato cream

Put the potato in the oven for 50 minutes at 200°c. When soft, put the potato flesh into a blender with the cream and 50g butter. Blend until smooth.

For the miso and lime beurre blanc

Boil the fish stock until reduced by half, and then add the cream and boil again until reduced by half. Add the cold butter, cut into small cubes, to the stock and combine with a stick blender. When the beurre blanc is smooth, add the miso paste and the zest of the lime.

For the halibut

Heat the clarified butter in a frying pan. Put the halibut in the pan and cook for about 5 minutes until golden brown, then turn over and cook for a further 1-2 minutes on the other side.

For the garnish

Cook the shiitake in a pan with the sea aster, chicken stock and some butter. Season with salt and pepper.

To serve

Place a spoonful of the shiitake mixture onto the plate, lay the halibut fillet over that and top with the sweet potato cream and a drizzle of the miso and lime beurre blanc.

Nose to TAIL

Butcheries in The Hague don't come more holistic than this; Nico and Sonja Englebert run Stijlslagerij Englebert to exacting standards to produce top quality meat for their shop.

The name Stijlslagerij Englebert is based on both the neighbourhood and the people who established it. The 'stijl period' of the twentieth century informed the architecture in The Hague that surrounds the butchery, which Nico and Sonja Englebert established more than 30 years ago. Their approach is best described as nose to tail; using the whole animal after slaughter means there's little waste and more traditional products can be created from the offal and other overlooked parts of the animal.

A big part of the range comes from Texel beef and lamb which has been selected and certified 'Waddengoud'. Waddengoud is a foundation that strictly controls the origins of local products from the Wadden, such as honey from the Black Bee, cranberries, and Texel lamb. Stijlslagerij Englebert is the only shop with the Waddengoud certificate in the whole of the South Holland province, and Nico drives to Texel every fortnight to pick up his meat directly from the slaughterhouse.

The Texel beef is sourced from Werner Drost, a farmer who guarantees excellent quality meat from Piedmontese cattle including prime cuts like cote de boeuf, T-bone, entrecote and rib-eye. For Texel lamb, Carlo Veeger supplies shoulder, cutlets and racks only from female Texelaar lambs, which carry the flavours of the salty grass of the Islay. Nico and Sonja make sure that the farmers they work with don't use unnatural products to feed their livestock, which are raised in free-range conditions. It's also important to them that the slaughter is done in stress-free circumstances, so they work with Cor Boschma who is "more than a skilled slaughterer; he maintains the relationship with the farmers on the Islay and also takes care of the animal's welfare in Texel."

For their pork, the Engleberts chose award-winning Livar for its authentic, honest and artisan principles and animals that are raised with respect for their natural behaviour and environment. Stijlslagerij Englebert have also received acknowledgement from the Italian ambassador for their Italian products including authentic Parma ham. Championing great products from home and abroad, the shop also stocks several Dutch cheeses; Boerenkaas from Marije van de Poel, and Cheese Affineurs Van Tricht from Antwerpen are just a few of the big names. Stijlslagerij Englebert is a butchers that does things properly and is proud to work from end to end when it comes to meat for your dinner table.

Stijlslagerij Englebert
DOUBLE TEXEL LAMB BURGER

The Texel lamb used in Nico and Sonja's butchery is certified 'Waddengoud' meaning you can be sure of its origins, which give the tender meat the flavour of Islay's salty grass, where the animals graze.

Preparation time: 15 minutes | Cooking time: 25 minutes | Serves: 4

Ingredients

600g minced lamb

100g crushed walnuts

2 sprigs of coriander, chopped

10g salt

20g Merguez herbs

8 slices of streaky bacon

50g feta cheese

Drizzle of honey

1 sprig of flat leaf parsley

4 whole walnuts

Method

Mix the minced lamb with the crushed walnuts, coriander, salt and Merguez herbs. Make eight small flat burgers that weigh around 75g each. Make your crosses on a baking tray with the streaky bacon. Put one burger in the middle of each cross of streaky bacon and add the feta cheese, some honey and flat leaf parsley on top. Gently push the second burger onto it, then wrap the streaky bacon to form a cross on top.

Sear the double burgers on each side in a hot frying pan, then transfer them into an ovenproof dish. Preheat the oven to 175°c. On each double burger, place a whole walnut and drizzle a little bit of honey over the top and then cook them in the oven for about 25 minutes.

A perfect
COMBINATION

Spanish tapas and Portuguese petiscos provided the name and the menu at Tapisco, a new restaurant bringing Mediterranean sunshine to The Hague.

2018 saw the opening of Michelin-starred chef Marcel van der Kleijn's fourth restaurant in the centre of The Hague. The restaurant is housed in a beautiful old building on the Kneuterdijk, where De Vijf Vocalen – a bookstore over 300 years old – was previously based. Tapisco is inspired by the Iberian kitchens Marcel came across during his holidays in Spain and Portugal, and its name is a combination of Spanish tapas and Portuguese petiscos.

During lunch and dinner at Tapisco you can choose from a variety of tapas and petiscos, all of which are made to high standards from the best ingredients. 'Little pillows' filled with sea bream and radish, crispy chicken skin with mackerel and mayonnaise, and handmade vegetarian empanadas are just a few examples of the creations. Diners can pick their favourites from the menu, or enjoy a surprise meal with dishes served at random.

Staff will suggest a perfect wine pairing by the glass or bottle to complete the experience from a selection of the best Portuguese and Spanish wines. Most of the wine regions are represented and even the local different grape varieties are listed. All the wines of the famous winemaker Telmo Rodríquez appear in Tapisco's wine list, and as a tribute to him there is a huge painting on the wall called 'mapa compañía de vinos telmo rodríguez'.

It's not just the food and drink that create such a relaxed yet eclectic atmosphere though; Tapisco puts on a show for its visitors. At the chef's table, guests are seated on a raised bench looking into the open kitchen where you can see the cooks doing their work in fine detail. Behind the huge and iconic bar the bartenders mix classic cocktails with their own modern and personal touch under the jambon iberico (Spanish hams) that are hung there to mature.

The rest of the restaurant's interior is a combination of modern influences and antique furniture. Authentic hand-painted Spanish tiles adorn the floors and the kitchen, and a tribute to the former bookstore has been created along one wall with a bookcase full of antique books. To top it all off, a sunny terrace out the front provides the perfect spot to enjoy your glass of wine and plates of food and be happily transported to the Mediterranean.

Restaurant Tapisco

Restaurant Tapisco

CHILLED SOUP OF TOMATO, CANTALOUPE MELON AND PALAMÓS ANCHOVIES

Gazpacho is a classic and well-known dish in Spain, especially during the summer as a refreshment in hot weather. We've put a Tapisco twist on this dish, but have kept the standard and key ingredients of the original.

Preparation time: 45 minutes | Serves: 4

Ingredients

For the soup:

150g cantaloupe melon, diced small

150g tomato concassée (peeled, deseeded, and chopped tomatoes)

40ml Ruby Port

50ml chicken broth

30ml Arbequina olive oil

½ lime, juiced

Salt and pepper

To garnish:

Palamós anchovies

Arbequina olive oil

100g cantaloupe melon balls

Indian cress (garden nasturtium) flowers

Method

For the soup

Blend all the ingredients in a food processor until you have a smooth, elegant soup and then season with salt and pepper to taste. Chill the soup to 6°c in the fridge.

To serve

Transfer the cold soup into chilled small bowls or plates. Garnish with the anchovy fillets from Palamós – these are the very best – and dry or deep fry the bones to use as a garnish. Add the melon balls, drizzle over a few drops of the olive oil and finish with the Indian cress flowers.

Cantonese
CLASSICS

Amongst the hustle and bustle of Den Haag's busy Frederik Hendriklaan Street lies Dim Sum Restaurant Walong, a traditional Yum Cha restaurant offering the best of Cantonese cuisine.

Respect for heritage is something that runs deep in Den Haag, reflected in the city's longstanding buildings and businesses that have stood as part of the community for generations. Dim Sum Restaurant Walong is one such place, with a celebrated history dating back to 1938 that has been detailed in the records of Den Haag's Chamber of Commerce. Fast-forward to the present; Restaurant Walong epitomises everything we've come to love about Chinese dining, with high quality traditional dishes served in a vibrant, buzzing atmosphere. It's with this vision of the future and respect for the past that the owners have succeeded in bringing Restaurant Walong into the modern era where it has become a household name in the homes of many Den Haag residents.

Residing on the famous Frederik Hendriklaan shopping street, the hustle and bustle of the 'De Fred' is drawn inside by Restaurant Walong's open glass store front, creating a seamless blend of busy Dutch streetscape and authentic Chinese culture. Diners can enjoy Walong's quality service under the restaurant's 101 hanging lanterns or outside on the spacious terrace, and take their dishes from the traditional centre turntables.

Among the restaurants clientele are staff from the Statenkwartierquarter's surrounding Asian embassies, demonstrating the authenticity and continuing quality of Walong's nearly century-old restaurant and recipes.

Keeping in line with the restaurant's emphasis on traditional flavours and practices, the recipes featured on Walong's menu have been put together by the owner and head chef's extensive knowledge of the five regional arts at the heart of Chinese cooking. These include the salty elements of the eastern Shanghai school, the sourness of northern Beijing cuisine, the spicy elements of Sichuan's western cooking, and – Walong's particular favourite – the Canton's southern school of cooking. Those visiting the restaurant can expect to enjoy an array of fried and steamed Cantonese dim sums in traditional Yum Cha style. Literally translating as 'drinking tea', Yum Cha reflects the English practice of taking high tea, and is another tradition that can be universally appreciated when family and friends come together to enjoy great company over great food, which the Dim Sum Restaurant Walong has become so famous for.

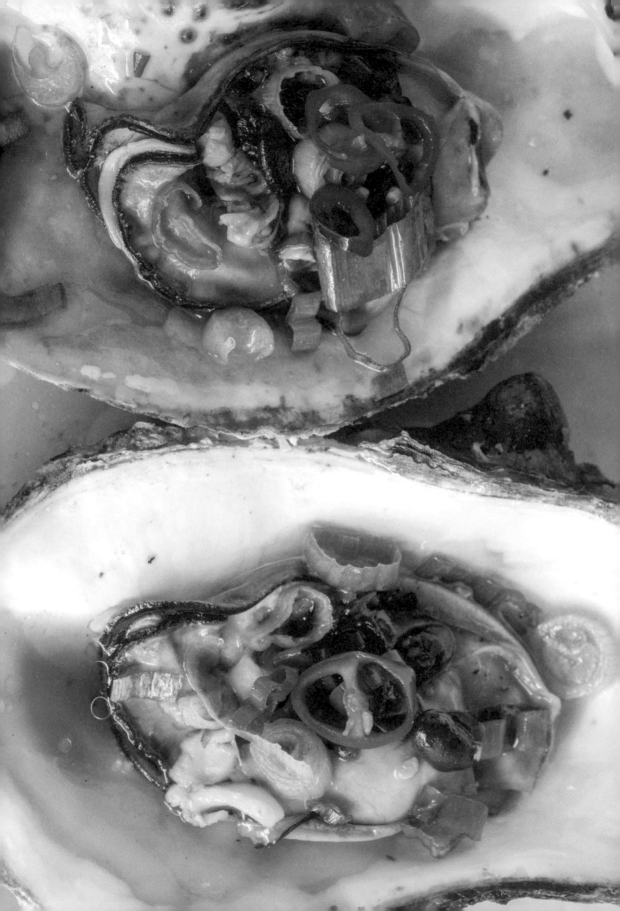

Walong
STEAMED OYSTERS
WITH BLACK BEAN

This recipe showcases the Chinese way of eating oysters: steamed with black beans and garnished with fried garlic, spring onion and drizzle of soy sauce dressing. Perfect for people who love oysters but can't stomach them raw!

Preparation time: 30 minutes | Cooking time: 15 minutes | Serves: 2

Ingredients

6-8 large fresh oysters, shell intact

For the sauce:

3 tbsp black beans, soaked in warm water for 30 minutes then drained

½ tbsp oyster sauce

½ tbsp chopped fresh garlic

1 tbsp corn starch, dissolved in 3 tbsp water

For the garnish:

3 tbsp vegetable oil

2 tbsp chopped fried garlic

2 tbsp chopped spring onion

1 red chilli pepper, thinly sliced

3 tbsp light soy sauce

Method

Scrub the oysters clean and then crack them open and rinse in cold water. Drain well. Combine the ingredients for the sauce in a bowl and then add one teaspoon of the mixture to each of the oysters.

Set up a steamer pan, fill it with water and bring it to the boil on high heat. Put one plate of oysters in the steamer and cover with the lid. Gently steam the oysters for about 3-5 minutes, depending on the size of the oysters. Carefully remove the plate from the steamer and immediately transfer the oysters to a serving dish.

To serve

In a wok, heat the oil until it reaches smoking point. Slowly and carefully drizzle hot oil over the oysters.

Garnish with fried garlic, spring onion, chilli and soy sauce and then serve immediately.

A design FOR LIFE

Bringing the elegance of a French bistro and the melting pot of New York cuisine together, Walter Benedict is a place of comfort and class in The Hague's historic centre.

When Bas and Jan-Willem decided to make a move into The Hague's diverse and innovative food scene, it took more than a year for them to discover the perfect venue. Good things come to those who wait, though, and when they spotted the beautiful shop front on Denneweg they just had to do something with the venue. Six months later, the renovated café bistro opened its doors. The concept has grown with its popularity, and Walter Benedict continues to accommodate locals, who were delighted to have an independent new eatery join the line-up in the heart of the city, as well as lots of tourists throughout the year.

Beyond the inviting windows and arched entrance, Walter Benedict is a warm and welcoming combination of classic French bistro and modern comfort. Bas and Jan-Willem's strong interest in design shines through in the exposed brick, wooden table tops, cabinets glittering with glassware and bright with greenery, and the marble bar atop glazed tiling: it's a feast for the eyes as well as the stomach. Views out to the busy street or through to the courtyard at the back of the building are great backdrops to a long lunch, late breakfast or evening meal.

Food is served all day at Walter Benedict, cultivating a relaxed atmosphere even in the hustle and bustle of The Hague's busy centre. The menu draws on both French and American influences, accompanied by an extensive wine menu from which many are available by the glass, to pair perfectly with charcuterie, cheese platters, seafood or steak tartare over dinner. Bistro classics will please carnivores and vegetarians alike, while over brunch and lunch the European staples take a leaf out of the Big Apple's book – think blueberry pancakes, cheesecake and of course, eggs benedict – to satisfy all appetites.

Bas and Jan-Willem also own and run Café Franklin in The Hague, with the same ethos of bringing cultures together over great food and drink and a lively yet laid-back atmosphere to enjoy. Investing time to innovate – in terms of design, cuisine and staff training – helps them to build places where people feel at home yet are inspired by original and authentic touches. The owners began their businesses because they love creating this kind of hospitality with people who also love what they do, and provide fun and genuine dining experiences across all aspects of The Hague's eclectic food and drink scene.

Walter Benedict

Photography by Myrthe Slootjes

Walter Benedict
EGGS BENEDICT

Whatever the season, whatever your mood, eggs benedict are always a good idea!

Preparation time: approx. 30 minutes | Cooking time: 5 minutes | Serves: 4

Ingredients

For the hollandaise sauce:

400ml white wine

600ml natural vinegar

400ml sushi vinegar

500g shallot, cut into rings

1 bay leaf

6 peppercorns

40g sugar

½ bunch of tarragon

300g egg yolk (about 12 yolks)

50g butter, cubed

Salt, to taste

For the brioche and poached eggs:

350ml natural vinegar

8 eggs

4 brioche buns

500g ham (minimum 8 slices)

½ a bundle of chives, finely chopped

Method

For the hollandaise sauce

Put the wine, natural vinegar, sushi vinegar, shallot rings, bay leaf, peppercorns, sugar and tarragon into a saucepan. Let the mixture boil down until you have about 200ml left. Strain the vinegar reduction through a sieve into a clean bowl. Sit the bowl over a pan of boiling water (to make a bain-marie) and add the egg yolk to the bowl. Whisk until you have a thick and airy sauce. Remove from the heat and add the cubes of butter one by one until all the butter is incorporated. Add salt to taste. Pour the hollandaise sauce into another clean bowl and cover with foil. Set aside in a warm place.

For the brioche and poached eggs

Preheat the oven to 180°c. Using a high-sided saucepan, heat four litres of water with the natural vinegar to 95°c. Break the eggs into separate coffee cups or ramekins, and when the water reaches the correct temperature use these to slide the eggs into the water one by one. Make sure you add them quickly for best results. Poach the eggs for 4 minutes. Meanwhile, cut the brioche buns in half (horizontally) and then place the brioche and slices of ham on an ovenproof plate. Put the plate into the preheated oven for 3-4 minutes. The brioche and ham are ready when both are golden brown.

To plate

Put two halves of brioche bun on one plate and cover each with a slice of ham. Use a skimmer to gently lift the poached eggs out of the pan, drain well, and then transfer to the bun on top of the ham. Gently stir the hollandaise sauce and then top each egg with a spoonful. Finish your eggs benedict with a pinch of fresh chopped chives and enjoy.

The DIRECTORY

These great businesses have supported the making of this book; please support and enjoy them.

André Kerstens BV

Kazernestraat 112
2514CW Den Haag
Telephone: +31 70 427 8321
Website: www.Andrékerstens.nl

Dutch importer of wines and spirits since 1880. In the assortment you will find bottles from France, Portugal and Spain and a small selection of other countries.

BIT Grill & Café

Buitenhof 39
2513 AH Den Haag
Telephone: +31 70 790 0032
Website: www.bitgrill.nl

Casual dining from breakfast to a late dinner on the ground floor of Hotel Corona, featuring steaks, burgers and rib roasts from the Josper grill.

Restaurant Basaal

Dunne Bierkade 3
2512 BC Den Haag
Telephone: +31 70 427 6888
Website:
www.restaurantbasaal.nl

Bib Gourmand restaurant that combines Dutch cuisine with French-style cooking as well as international influences, situated on one of The Hague's most beautiful canals.

Bites & Stories

Telephone: +31 61 094 3148
Website:
www.bitesandstories.com

Discover The Hague through its bites and stories on food, wine and beer tours guided by local experts!

Brooklyn Burgers & Steaks

Night Club
Strandweg 43
2586 JL Den Haag
The Netherlands
Telephone: +31 70 350 2068
Website:
www.brooklynscheveningen.nl

First class American-style burgers, steaks and ribs in a relaxed restaurant setting.

Café Franklin

Valkenbosplein 24
2563 CC Den Haag
Telephone: +31 70 785 1412
Website: www.cafefranklin.nl

Bar and café at the heart of a bustling neighbourhood, putting flavours from around the world, local and international beers, and relaxed socialising on the menu.

Restaurant Calla's

Laan van roos en doorn 51 a
2514 BC Den Haag
Telephone: +31 70 345 5866
Website:
www.restaurantcallas.nl

Michelin-starred restaurant at the forefront of fine dining in The Hague, focusing on fresh and seasonal ingredients, with a contemporary approach to Dutch cuisine.

Restaurant de Tapperij

Atjehstraat 66
2585 VL Den Haag
Telephone: +31 70 352 3998
Website:
www.restaurantdetapperij.nl

One of The Hague's oldest café restaurants, serving traditional Dutch cuisine in a nostalgic setting made with fresh, seasonal produce and a modern approach.

Didong Indonesisch eten

2e Sweelinckstraat 115
2517 GW Den Haag
Telephone: +31 70 364 9887
Website: www.didong.nl

Traditional Indonesian cooking with a Dutch twist.

Restaurant Elea

Herenstraat 83-85
2282 BS Rijswijk
Telephone: +31 70 214 3860
Website:
www.restaurantelea.nl

Haute cuisine restaurant with a modern and innovative cooking style, where you can enjoy dishes with a subtle Greek influence.

Gransjean Wijnen & Delicatessen

Bankastraat 12
2585 EN Den Haag
Telephone: +31 70 350 3980
Website: www.gransjean.nl

Delicatessen stocked with wines and delicious products from local producers as well as from all over the world.

Marius Jouw Wijnvriend

Piet Heinstraat 93
2518 CD Den Haag
Telephone: +31 70 363 3100
Website:
www.jouwwijnvriend.nl

Welcoming and knowledgeable wine merchant with a wide range of directly imported wines, focusing on small producers and European varieties.

Naga Thai

Frederik Hendriklaan 264
2582 Bn Den Haag
Telephone: +31 70 355 8857
Website: www.nagathai.nl

Traditional Thai kitchen with a modern and homely ambiance where you can relax and enjoy authentic good food, reasonably priced and full of flavour.

OCEANS Beach House

Strandweg Tent 32
2586 JK Den Haag
The Netherlands
Telephone: +31 70 350 2073
Website:
www.oceansschevenigen.nl

Great seafood, cocktails and Champagne served in a modern and sophisticated beach house.

Ohana Poké

Prinsestraat 18
2513 CD Den Haag
Telephone: +31 70 737 0580
Website: www.ohanapoke.nl

Ohana Poké serves visually stunning and tasty food, in a hip and minimalistic environment, made with love from sustainable and socially responsible products.

The Old Jazz

Aert van der Goesstraat 7
Den Haag
Telephone: +31 70 205 0541
Website: www.theoldjazz.nl

Family-run, French inspired café bar reinvented from one of the city's most beloved 'brown cafés'.

Restaurant Oogst

Denneweg 10B
2514 CG Den Haag
Telephone: +31 70 360 9224
Website:
www.restaurantoogst.nl

Focused on fresh ingredients and modern French cuisine with Dutch influences, Restaurant Oogst turns bountiful harvests into seasonal feasts.

Pâtisserie Jarreau

Van Hoytemastraat 42
2596 ER Den Haag
Telephone: +31 70 324 8719
Website: www.jarreau.nl

Award-winning patisserie specialising in macarons, offering workshops and creating innovative new seasonal treats as well as French classics.

Portfolio

Prinsestraat 36
2513 CD Den Haag
Telephone: +31 70 219 9691
Email:
info@portfolio-restaurant.nl

New, innovative and internationally influenced restaurant.

Stijlslagerij Englebert

Goudsbloemlaan 83
2565 CP Den Haag
Telephone: +31 70 360 6811
Website: www.stijlslagerij.nl

Butchery in The Hague selling certified top-quality meats and other products.

Restaurant Tapisco

Kneuterdijk 11
2514 EM Den Haag
Telephone: +31 70 204 5006
Website:
www.restauranttapisco.nl

Restaurant which combines Spanish and Portuguese cuisine in a Mediterranean atmosphere, with an iconic cocktail bar.

Seafoodbar Vigo

Aert van der Goesstraat 9
Den Haag
Telephone: +31 70 205 0273
Website: restaurantvigo.nl

Seafoodbar Vigo is a contemporary seafood bar promising the best quality fish and dining experience in The Hague.

Restaurant Walong

Frederik Hendriklaan 286
2582 BN Den Haag
Telephone: +31 70 355 2146
Website:
www.restaurantwalong.nl

Offering fresh dim sum and authentic Chinese cuisine in a central location on 'De Fred' with a warm and cosy atmosphere.

Walter Benedict

Denneweg 69a
2514 CE Den Haag
Telephone: +31 70 785 3745
Website:
www.walterbenedict.nl

French-American style food in a classic bistro setting, with a rustic feel and an extensive wine list to complement the lunch and evening menus.